Street Food Soliloquy

Starting and Running a UK Street Food Business

To Barny.

Because you made me tea.

First published 2015

D1355493

Contents

Introduction

Congratulations, the hard part is basically over. If you have got as far as reading this then you probably already have a fair idea of what you would like to do and are pretty keen to get started. Hopefully the collected wisdom of us, The Jabberwocky, will be able to help you get your act together and out there selling street food.

The Jabberwocky, our business, was founded by surprise in early 2011 when we realised that we no longer wanted to work for other people. Present at that moment was Barny, who was my boyfriend at the time. He had given up teaching Chemistry at secondary school to become a chef a few years earlier. Having made it to head chef he was at a bit of a loose end. The only two options for progression from there were to acquire a restaurant or go work in Michelin Starred fine dining establishments.

Fine dining means working long, antisocial hours in surprisingly small, eerily lit, sweaty rooms with many bad-tempered men, all of whom are mostly stressed, nearly all the time. A dream job for some: especially when you can occasionally catch a glimpse of some celebrity chef flouncing through the kitchen, trying to justify his name on the sign; but apparently not Barny's cup of tea[1].

I was working in a dead end job at a games company, providing in-game customer support to people who had become stuck in a hole, or whose dragon kept vanishing while they were trying to kill it. The world of online gaming is a strange and magical place, but on the whole it gets really dull when you have asked the 18th person in a row to hang on where they are while you reset the hoard of angry townspeople so that they can attack again.

We wanted to do something that was ours. Something where you could sweep the work off your desk, fling your notice at your boss and exit to jubilant and admiring applause, safe in the knowledge that you

---

[1] Unlike tea, which is very much his cup of tea.

would never need to work for a CV requiring, reference checking multinational again.

This is how we did it.

I've always felt that the best way to learn how to do something is to have a stab at it yourself. You get hands-on experience that way, but then you also get to make all your own mistakes. As mistakes are expensive when you're trying to earn a living, I want to take some of the legwork out for you.

The title is a giveaway, but the plan is to show you how to start a street food business, mostly so that you can avoid the mistakes we made and become successful, stupidly wealthy and even more good looking. There are also a lot of tricks we have learnt along the way, from our own research and from getting it right. That is all in here too. We already have one of the most exhaustive guides on the web about getting started in street food, so this is designed to provide some detailed information and give you a solid, slightly more organised grounding so that you feel confident in taking the leap and getting started. This is the book I wish had been around when we started.

Back in 2011, street food did not really exist at all. There were already lots of people out there cooking interesting things, but the media had not found out how photogenic your dinner could be, and we thought that "street food" would be a super cool name for our new product.

We proceeded to make a large number of mistakes, the most magnificent of which will be collected here for your pleasure, enlightenment and titillation. Eventually, sometime later, we were able to ditch our full time jobs, hoist the main sail on the van and venture out into self-employment.

The Jabberwocky today is a high-sided VW LT31, of the kind they just don't make any more, in deep Brunswick green. We call him the Beast. Together we travel all over Warwickshire and the Midlands from our base in Leamington Spa, selling toasties made with locally baked bread, some amazing cheeses from across Europe and a whole host of local game, meat, produce and vegetables.

Throughout this process I've doggedly maintained our blog to try and document our progress as a way of helping others and to satisfy my desire to somehow crowbar some writing into my job. This is now my contribution to the industry that has given me more satisfaction than any other, in the hope that it will keep going, that folks will want to develop new food and that we will be able to retire early.

Chapter 1

Basics before you Start

We all have to start somewhere. If you are considering setting up some sort of food business then wrap your eyes around this chapter, take notes and underline significant parts with highlighter, because everyone watching will be terribly impressed. At the end of it you will hopefully know if this business is for you, and that might save you a pile of money, heartbreak and time further down the line. This part contains all the facts you should need to decide if street food is for you.

What Is Street Food?

Street food is selling high quality, hot food outdoors. As with many emerging words the concept is not terribly well defined yet, but it's probably easier to define in contrast to other kinds of outdoor catering.

Mobilers are probably the longest established breed of outdoor caterer. They are typically characterised by the white trailer, and serve uncomplicated food that is bought pre- prepared and then cooked and served from inside the unit. You find them on high streets, at car boot sales and in laybys. Typical food will consist of a mass-produced burger, the bacon butty and chips and jacket potatoes.

Festival Caterers generally trade from much larger units, with a large staff and a focus on getting the food out as fast as possible. The quality here varies greatly, but is now rapidly improving since its precocious little sibling hit the scene. Generally the food here is also mass produced and then heated and served on site, although there is much more variety than in the white trailer and you will often find international food offerings. These units are often centrally owned and run by managers and staff following orders, rather than being owner-operated.

Finally in contrast to these two you have us: **Street Food**; the newest alfresco dining option. These units are predominantly owned and run by the person serving the food, they are focussed around one single product and the aim is to serve the best possible. The meat is sourced locally, nthing is mass produced and the emphasis is on quality ingredients. Uniquely, street food traders have the opportunity to straddle all three branches of outdoor catering. This sort of food was born in the recession, when people wanted to eat interesting food but not pay restaurant prices for it. Now that we're establishing a foothold in many towns and cities the idea is here to stay, and will keep on growing as long as people keep on finding interesting food to sell.

How Much Does It Cost to Get Set Up?

Setup costs vary wildly depending on what sort of unit you want to trade from, but if you are looking to get out there and trading as quickly and cheaply as possible then you *can* get set up for around £1000. It won't be future-proof, it's not recommended, but it can be done. Let me break it down for you.

I'm going to base this on burgers/hotdog/pulled pork – simple meat in a bun, if you catch my drift. This is the cheapest option to set up, but please don't be fooled into rushing in and doing it. Do what you love.

A second hand (LPG) catering grill	£345
A flimsy gazebo	£70
Second-hand handwash unit	£50
Gas bottle, regulator and hoses	£100
Folding table	£35
Food temperature probe	£6
Plastic tablecloth	£5
Fire Extinguisher	£30
Fire Blanket	£5
Menu Board	£5
Cold box & cold packs	£40
Tongs	£5
Napkins to serve meat-in-a-bun	£3
Tubs for salad and sides	£5
Colour-coded chopping mats	£5
Gas safe check for grill	£50
Cleaning products	£40
Public Liability Insurance	£150
Basic Food Hygiene Certificate	£30
20l Water Bottle	£15
Catering First Aid Kit	£5
Total	**£998**

That constitutes your absolute bear minimum to be able to trade, but you will find life hard. Equipment will break, everything will blow away in the slightest gust of wind and sales will not be especially good. There is, after all, a good reason why most of us spend a lot more than that.

The list is really intended to give you a basic idea of what you need, and guide prices for some things you have to have, most of which are legal necessities. Talk to your local environmental health officer to see what the exact requirements are for your area. See the health and safety section for more details.

For £3000 you can have a decent quality setup that should last you the season. You will then need a fund for applications, so that you can actually find somewhere to trade. £5000, spent carefully, should see you into making money out of the business rather than putting it in. For trailer and van setups simply add the price of the fully kitted out unit (and in the case of a van, road tax, MOT and insurance) onto this – expect to spend that saved gazebo money on repairs, sundries and, eventually, a gazebo.

If you are planning on doing your own van or trailer conversion then the budget is in your hands, but even with both hands firmly round the throat of whomever is doing your accounts I wouldn't expect much change from £8000, assuming you do the work yourself.

What Skills Do You Need to get started?

Street fooders come from all walks of life, meaning we all have different skills and talents, and focus on different aspects. The only thing that unites us all is that we can drive. Before we get onto anything else, you have to drive and you have to own a car at the very least. Everything else is negotiable, but you cannot carry this kind of kit around on the bus. Good. I'm going to assume that you can drive and do own a car for the sake of not needing to add it at the end of every sentence, so if you can't drive and don't have a business partner who can, you need to get that sorted first.

The more of the skills below you have, the easier the ride will be. If you can't tick off any of them then bear in mind that ridiculous enthusiasm will still get you a very long way, and stuff about not being able to teach old dogs is hogwash.

Top five street food skills

1. **Being able to cook.** Specifically, being able to cook the thing you want to sell well enough that people will buy it. If you consider yourself to be something of a health hazard in the kitchen, you have a long road ahead of you, my friend.
2. **Business know-how.** Starting and running a company, managing your time, selling yourself and keeping your budget under control, along with dozens of other useful, semi-related soft skills. Any tiny shred of knowledge here will be a huge advantage.
3. **DIY and Car repairs.** Something will break right when you urgently need it not to, so if you can fix it, you are onto a winner. As an added bonus, good-looking home-made shabby-chic hipster junk just screams street food.
4. **Social Media, design and Web knowhow.** I know, having all three would be lovely, but any experience (and contacts) in the jumbled field of marketing will be really useful further down the line.
5. **A bit of maths, and a bit of English.** You will need fast, accurate mental arithmetic unless you have time to deal with a till. Adding £4+£3.50x2+£1+£5 and then returning £3 when you are given a £20 is much faster than letting a till tell you. There is also your accounting, where those terrified of numbers get to truly experience hell – or pay a bookkeeper. Your written English will come up when you write to clients trying to get business, putting copy on your website or in your interaction on social media. It doesn't have to be Shakespeare, but getting a bit of punctuation in there will change the reader's attitude towards you dramatically. People do not retweet or share a misspelling.

Top 5 street food character traits

1. **Enthusiasm & Optimism.** Starting a street food business will be a lot easier if you want it badly, especially when everything goes wrong. I don't think you can do this without at least one major cock up (per week in some cases), so you can safely assume that every street fooder you see trading today has been at the point where they wanted to quit, but have stuck it out.
2. **Approachability.** It's a cliché, but you need to be a people person. Talking to people, generating rapport and

consequently securing repeat custom will make you money. Plus you will be way nicer to work with. For the rest of us, that is.

3. **Persuasion.** By this I mean both the ability to sell yourself and your product, which has a lot to do with good old fashioned enthusiasm, as well as the knack of being able to make other people want your unit at their festival and your food in their bellies. It's not exactly one that is heralded as a virtue, but it will come in ever so handy.

4. **A good palette.** You work in food, knowing what tastes good is dead useful.

5. **Improvisation & problem solving.** The inevitable catastrophes are not always the end of the road, so being able to think your way out of a tight spot is surprisingly useful.

Who should be a Street Food Vendor?

If you have just finished the list above and can confidently claim boundless quantities of everything listed then you should probably get cracking. Then again with a skill set like that you can probably achieve just about anything, so start by using your powers for Good in the world, and come back to street food later.

My point is that you don't need all those qualities to be successful. The only one I think is absolutely vital is that you are enthusiastic about making great food. I've met enough traders who are happy to make a living out of it, but no longer get any enjoyment from doing it. It makes it easy to scrimp on quality, because money/recession/time/effort (delete excuse as applicable). If you want this badly enough (and have a car), you can do this.

Of course nobody knows what the future holds; you can't know that you will always have the same passion and hunger you have now. Luckily this isn't a life sentence. As long as you want it now; and realistically for the next 2 years at least, then you have enough to be getting on with. You can always sell the business and do something else later.

What are the Benefits of Working in Street Food?

I had a conversation with a customer on New Street, Birmingham once which started like many do. He was waiting for his toastie to cook, and asked if there was a lot of money in street food. I told him what I tell everyone when they ask this: that there is a lot less than they think. Usually this is followed by questions about whether I'm sure, or disbelief, or confusion as to how we could possibly not be making a small fortune. Instead, this guy asked me why, if the money was so bad, I was doing it at all.

I love my job. Job satisfaction has always been my end goal in the working world, and for me this is the ultimate in satisfactory activities. I told him this.

But I didn't make any money, how could I possibly have job satisfaction?

And so we went backwards and forwards, with the guy absolutely insistent that making big bucks was either equal to or better than enjoying your job.

You can make a living in street food. It requires no formal qualifications (other than a food hygiene certificate - £30 and available online) it is ideal for anyone who fancies their chances and wants to be their own boss. It is not, as we are so often told, a license to print money. If your primary goal is to get rich quick then this is really not for you. Out of your three outdoor catering branches – Street Food, Mobilers and Festival Caterers – it will probably sit somewhere in the middle in terms of turnover, but the hours are long, hard and decidedly antisocial.

So why do I like doing it?

Beside my history in catering I am an office worker; 9-5, Monday to Friday, overtime, tea-breaks, meetings, conference calls, reporting, appraisals and customer service. I used to crave any break to the monotony. I'd yearn for excitement; the next holiday, the end of the working day, lunch. When asked what I wanted to do at the weekends

I'd hopefully say "an adventure". We'd do a National Trust, or go see friends, or change gas supplier.

Street Food is an adventure. We have jumped into the driving seat of a great green Beast and gone careering off into the wilds of Warwickshire. We go to places nearby that I never knew existed. We roam festivals, visit all kinds of weird and wonderful activities and get to try food and meet people from all over the world. Better than that: wherever we go people are pleased to see us. I don't think there is another job like it.

For Barny, kitchen veteran and passionate cook, the benefits are even more tangible. He gets to cook, which he loves, and then – unlike almost every other job in the business – he actually gets to serve the food as well. Most chefs who go into the business will say it's because they love food, but seeing as they very rarely get to eat what they make, I think they really do it for the joy of giving people food. From inside a fluorescent lit, boiling hot back room you then don't really get a great impression of the customer outside. We actually get to meet them.

Not only that, but rather than being shut in the back (most chefs are far too scruffy during service to be allowed into the restaurant) he has forsaken the kitchen for the great outdoors; the same view of a wall, grill and fridges for the endless variety of a hundred new locations and the pomp and circumstance of the restaurant trade for the entirely unpretentious alfresco dining. Ok, street food is not entirely without pretention, but there is no food more honest than when it's cooked right there in front of you.

Don't do this to get rich, do this to improve your quality of life. Sometimes it will rain, and that sucks, but when the sun is shining and a sceptic comes back to say that actually they really enjoyed your dish then you will know you made the right decision.

Do you have to give up your Job?

Increasingly as times remain hard, people are looking for interesting ways to make a little on the side. Street food happens to mix beautifully with a nine-to-five job, meaning that you can easily hold down both, providing you don't need sleep.

Most of the markets and festivals you will initially encounter will be in the evening or at weekends. That's when the leisure-inclined public are most likely to be on the prowl for gourmet offerings, and you will find that the average spend is higher and more frequent than at any other time. You certainly don't need to chuck in your job the moment you buy a van. Both Barny and I had full time jobs for the whole of our first full year and well into our second. Eventually I gave up my job because, looking at our planned events for the year ahead, I didn't have time for it anymore.

It is a lot of hard work. There were a few weeks shortly before I quit when I didn't actually have any day where I wasn't either at work or out in the van. Paperwork for the business had to be done in the evenings. Much tea was consumed. More than usual, even. Looking back, I'm really not sure how we still fitted everything in back then, as we are still busy every day even without the inconvenience of having to show up for work 5 times a week.

Should I get a Partner?

More than half of the street food vendors I know run the business as a couple. We started out when we had been going out for five years, and now we're married. As with all good partnerships it's the division of labour and the shared desire for a similar end result that will decide whether this is going to work, regardless of whether you are a couple, business partners or friends. When it comes to food, Barny has the final say – the 51% share, effectively. When it comes to online and marketing, I have the casting vote.

Obviously if you are friends or a couple it might well change your relationship. You may find that talking about business becomes strangely alluring (don't ask me why) or that you wake up in the middle of the night with an idea you really need to share. Luckily for us, conversations about this business are still interesting, and quite frequently the topic of hours of debate. It might have brought us closer as a couple, but either way, it gives us something to talk about.

Working as a couple also has other benefits: If the business starts to take off and you are still in full time employment then one of you might be able to drop hours or quit completely while the other carries on with work. Especially in that first year, while you are still separating the good events from the bad, a solid monthly income can be really useful.

Generally speaking, the old adage about two heads being better than one holds true. There are two of you who are (hopefully) equally committed to the business. This means two of you to divide up the boring jobs, get the repetitive jobs out the way and take responsibility when things go wrong (which is **not** the same as blaming the other person). If you get a second unit to capitalise on your inevitable success further down the line, there are two people who can each take a team to an event.

I should stress though that you will end up spending a lot of your time together. Especially if you are working *and* living with a partner. It may not work for everyone, and does take some getting used to. When I eventually gave up full time work a few months after Barny we did start arguing more, but then again we also get to share our successes and work through problems together.

I would suggest that there are two strategies here, but you will need to find a method that works for you:

1. You both share the same goal and want to get there in the same way. Effectively equal partners, although I would strongly suggest a division of labour based of what you're good at. This means any discussions will usually be resolved to the satisfaction of both sides, and tough decisions can be made as a team.
2. One of you is in charge, the other one is 2nd in command. You effectively make one partner the managing director, who has to make the final call on everything. The other partner can stay in work, support the business and help out where required.

If you do choose option one, which is undoubtedly the hardest one to work, I would advise a quick stock take of your prospective partner and yourself. This is what you are looking for:

- Similar work ethic (so that you are not doing all the work while they watch)
- Complimentary skills (if you are both in the kitchen you may have too many cooks)
- Similar goals and ambitions (you're working towards the same thing)
- The same general attitude in life (you will solve problems in a similar way)

Can you make a lot of Money?

The amount you will make is almost exactly proportionate to the effort invested. If you do one event each week where you make £500, you will earn £500. If you do 4 events, you will earn £2000. It will take time to work out which events are worth your effort and which ones aren't, but the simple answer is that yes, you can make quite a lot of money, depending very much on your personal definition of "a lot".

But, and this is a fairly sizable but; there is not nearly as much *profit* in it as you might think. Food – the ingredients we use – have increased in price significantly over the last few years. Most people have a perception of wholesale ingredients costing next-to-nothing. It's not the case, especially with the kind of products you will want to use. Good quality ingredients are a lot more expensive than the cheapest ones.

As street food traders we have the luxury of not trading from a bricks-and-mortar business, so the actual costs are lower, but out of every unit you shift, on top of the ingredients, you will also need to pay:

- Pitch fees
- Packaging
- Gas / Electricity to cook it, chill it or illuminate it
- Petrol to get you there
- Staff costs
- Equipment upkeep & wear & tear
- Wastage
- Insurance

Everything after that, you keep... apart from income tax. And corporation tax. Unless you hit the VAT threshold, in which case a further 20% goes in VAT. Wham, bam thank you taxman.

Basics Before You Start – Summary

Hopefully that gives you an idea of what you are getting yourself into. I'm not trying to sell you the idea of starting up in street food; I'm trying to be honest, so that you can make an informed decision about whether or not this whole excursion into mobile catering is for you. We love it because it's an adventure, no day is quite like the last and you are master of your own destiny. You may find that there are other things, or no part of that which appeal.

What follows is largely based on our journey through the first four years of working in street food. I've pulled out all the important parts and explained the things we got wrong, so that hopefully you won't make the same mistakes.

Right now, ask yourself:

With all that in mind, do I still want to do it?

Yes, yes, yes? If after reading that last part you are more excited than ever and know that this would be an amazing way to make a living then read on. Good luck and don't forget to come and say hi if you see us out and about.

Umm? Write down why you want to start a street food business. This is a surprisingly big commitment, and if you can't name a good few personal reasons why you want to get involved think it through again. Get out and see some street food markets, talk to traders and ask what they get out of it, read our story and see if that helps with the up and down feelings you're having (there are ups and downs, it's perfectly natural). You can even try and get some work experience with a street fooder by offering free labour for a few outings. Most traders will be surprisingly receptive to the offer.

No. If it isn't for you, it isn't for you. I'm glad we could help avoid a potentially expensive crisis. Please still support street food, now you know how much work goes into it: the industry needs enlightened fans like you.

Chapter 2

Getting Started

You have made the commitment, so this is what you need to do next. Most of these jobs are only fun if you have a serious paperwork fetish, but hang in there: once you're out the other side it's just food and glory.

Timeline for Trading

These are all the jobs you need to get done before you can actually start to trade. Here is the approximate time which these jobs are likely to take, but to be honest this is a labour of love, you need to take as long as it needs. However, if you want to be trading soon, and have plenty of spare time in the evenings, I think you could realistically work to this schedule. Each job is addressed in detail in the next two chapters. I think this is the most sensible chronological order, but not the order we subsequently did it in.

As a result of this three key points: Food, name and unit are not in that order. Just so you're prepared.

Job	Suggested Time Frame (in weeks from now)	Time spent on activity (in approx. hours)	Tick Box!
Decide that you are going to do this	Now.	Yes? Good. Done.	
Work out your budget	This week	2	
Write a business plan	This week	3	
Decide on your food	This week	1	
Pick a name	This week	2	
Food hygiene certificate	This week	3	
Set up a company	Next week	2	
Register with the local authority	Next week	1	
Choose your Unit	Next week	1	
Collect events	Next Week	4	

Write an equipment list	Next Week	2	
Print & Read Safer Food, better business.	2 Weeks' time	1	
Go equipment shopping	2 Weeks' time	2	
Test-build unit	2 Weeks' time	3	
Test-cook food	2 Weeks' time	3	
Risk Assessment	2 Weeks' time	2	
Plan branding and logo	3 Weeks' time	3	
Set up social media	3 Weeks' time	2	
Apply for events	3 Weeks' time	3	
Gas Safe test	4 Weeks' time	1	
Pat tests	4 Weeks' time	1	
EHO inspection	4 Weeks' time	2	

Business Plan

In every good guide to starting a business, there is an extensive chapter on business plans. They are an important structural tool in your business and you will not get any sort of sensible investment without one. Everyone says so.

When we first started out, bright eyed and full of hope, I wrote one for starting a restaurant business. I never looked at it, referenced it or even thought about it again until I came to write this section. On the other hand, I wasn't trying to get a loan. We financed the Jabberwocky from savings and never needed to justify our project to anyone else outside our own heads; with the possible exception of a few friends and family who had great ideas for what we should do instead.

However our business had an odd structure to it already because of the blog, which predates both the van and the company. It already followed our exploits and provided structure to an otherwise distinctly ethereal project. So rather than suggesting you download yet another non-specific guide from the internet I'd recommend you write something that will help you set up this business, and can then be used as a business plan if you do need to approach a bank or lender for money. Don't worry about formatting, spelling or word count. No one is going to mark it; just get this in writing.

Most of the specifics will be covered in later chapters, so don't panic. That's pretty crucial for this whole project.

Contents of your Business Plan

- **A basic outline;** the so-called "Executive Summary". What you want to do, where you want to do it, how much you think is it going to cost. The more money you can invest, the easier this is going to be.
- **About the Directors.** Why are you are the best person to do this. Seriously, look at your own skills and work out why you are great for the job; Your can-do attitude, your winning smile, your post graduate in Street Food Economics of Northern Europe, whatever.
- **The Time line.** You know your schedule, so get a calendar and work out where you want to be in a month, in three months, in 6 months, in a year from now. List the jobs you plan to get done and the cash you will need to do them; see above for details. Remember that this is for you, not the bank, so be realistic.
- **Finances.** You know how much cash you need, so where is it all going to come from? At least the first £1000 will have to come from you before you can start taking anything back, remembering that on top of that you personally still need things like food, rent and heating. Set targets for how many events you want to do and how much money you want to make in the same way as before: 1 month, three months, 6 months, 1 year. Decide the types of event as well. Will you go

high cost, high profit festivals or low cost, low profit markets? Start slow and build? Or invest heavily and go in guns blazing?

- **Marketing Strategy.** What makes your business unique? Why will people eat your food? How will you keep them coming back? How will you get them interested in the first place? What was that bright idea you had at 3am two nights ago? Facebook, twitter, flyers, songs, samples and good old-fashioned conversation – think about how you're going to get your customers to - and it pains me to use the terminology - engage with your brand.
- **Any other information.** Add any other details that don't fit into previous categories at the end (see the rest of this chapter for details).

Business plans are often very long, very dull documents. If you only have one or two pages of A4 by this time, that's probably cool. It might mean you actually revisit it later, or use it as a foundation for something more structured and investible later on.

Our Journey

The tale of our street food van is not a model you should copy, as we did things in an odd order with no clear idea of what we were aiming for. It is a great way of showing you exactly how we did something, and why we came to do it in that manner. The tale of the Jabberwocky can therefore be found throughout the next few chapters, but can be easily avoided by skipping the italics.

January 2011

People fall into street food from all sorts of different places. For us the first step was deciding to start a food business. I thought perhaps a restaurant, Barny had been looking through pubs in the area and we both wanted something that would be uniquely ours. Most of these projects required a huge upfront investment of money we didn't have, and both of them would have left me doing a job that essentially amounted to waitressing.

I have no problem waiting tables; I've done it for most of my adult life. Meeting new people is fun, but restaurants had broken me in the past. The hours are long, the pay is poor and some customers - bless their inability to see past their own noses - are inclined to regard you as walking, talking furniture. There did not seem to be any sort of alternative for working in food, so we made enquires, visited several properties and hoped that some benevolent money-ridden industrialist would accidentally favour us in his will and then suffer an unexpected but swift demise.

We had already taken the first steps though. The project had a name. Somehow, that seemed important to us. Being as we didn't know what we were going to sell, how we were going to sell it or any of the other finer details, we settled on picking a name instead. Over the years I have given various explanations for how The Jabberwocky came about; the question comes up so frequently it's about time I made up a much more interesting origin, but it is what it is.

The mundane explanation is that we like the poem; the word has a strange and wonderful character to it and seems to stick in the mind. We had already excluded most of the more familiar Alice in Wonderland characters (white rabbits, Cheshire cats and so forth) because they were already so overused as to be dull.

At the age of 12 or 13 I had decided to teach myself the entire poem, as one does when preparing for the moody angst of teenage, and with the exception of a few words, which have become scrambled through the years, I still know it. The name sounded right: Interesting, vaguely familiar and, with the exception of people who think we sell Indian cuisine, quintessentially British; which was also a good description for Barny's food.

Choosing A Name

We are one of the few street fooders out there whose name does not have even the slightest connection to food. Funny or interesting are both good and ultimately memorable, but a name that is also a description will mean one fewer question the punter has to ask before buying. Your name will probably be your first opportunity to advertise your product, so putting the food in the title has huge, obvious benefits. If I were back in 2011 giving myself advice, I would not have recommended the Jabberwocky.

Assuming you know what you are planning to sell. Which we didn't. So we were going for the restaurant strategy instead, where your name is reminiscent of a theme rather than a meal. In street food though, I would aim as close to food as you can: **Make it memorable, keep your product in mind and try not to confuse people.**

If you call yourselves Bear Eats Food you are not tied to a product, you are referencing food and you have an automatic mascot or logo. Call yourself the Rare Rabbit Kitchen and you will be constantly asked if what you sell contains bunny.

If you already know what you will be selling, which hopefully you do, then that is where your name should come from. A clever pun is usually appreciated, but if we had called ourselves "The Toastie Van" from day one I have no doubt that things would have worked out differently.

Having said that; we are often recognised from places where we have never traded before. The name is effortlessly familiar, what with it being part of our collective literary consciousness. That doesn't stop it from being frequently mistaken for that guy of-off Star Wars: Jabba The Hut - Really more giant slug than guy, but who's counting.

If you do go for something recognisable then make sure you read up on copyright. Everything written in the 20th Century is still off limits, but anything where the author has been dead for more than 70 years is now in the public domain.

Choosing Your Unit
January 2011

The day we finally stumbled into street food was a freezing morning two days after I had written off a car on an icy road. We were out hunting for a replacement car and simultaneously following a couple of van auctions on ebay. Barny's new idea was to buy a van, convert it into a mobile kitchen and then cook food from there. We would be mainly event and wedding caterers, but could visit the occasional food festival as marketing. The idea seemed solid; Barny was a proper chef and event catering seemed pretty lucrative. We had already visited a few old VW campervans, and realised that Barny would never be able to stand up in them.

The auction we were following at the time was for a high-sided VW LT, the panel van version of the almost-iconic 80s camper we all know and love. It was bright yellow and had a full side of burger-based mural done in graffiti. Most importantly, it had a hatch and work surfaces. According to the largely factual if somewhat vague description (later found to be basically made up) the van was ready to trade and a steal at less than £2000.

Your Unit will probably be your first big financial investment when you go into street food. The road is littered with unexpected smaller costs, but you will need some kit to sell food from. There are three basic setups you can choose from in order to have a self-contained service area. If you take a stall at a produce or farmers market then you will usually be provided with a table and roof, in which case all you need is cooking equipment. At most other trading events you will be provided with a space, usually 3x3m (or multiples of that), and will have to bring and assemble everything you wish to have there by hand. These are your options.

Investing in a Van

In terms of assembly, a van is by far the simplest option. Your entire kitchen arrives ready to go, and most of the setup on-site is cosmetic. You won't have a support vehicle to worry about which then has to be parked (and paid for) elsewhere and retrieved at the end of the day.

For us it means that unlike many of our gazebo based counterparts, and even some trailers, we can comfortably get our single unit to two events in one day. Double eventing in any other setup can easily be solved by getting a full second unit, but that also means getting two sets of food for the same day, rather than just running the ingredients you didn't sell that lunchtime onwards to an evening service.

There are obvious downsides. Vans, especially those with character, are characterful because they are old. Age takes its toll on everything eventually, and that can happen at any time, especially when you are in a rush, or it's raining. Everyone who relies on a vehicle for their living has to accept that occasionally they will break down. Those of us who intentionally go out of our way to invest in a collection of rust and dreams just have to accept a greater proportion of our time will be spent huddled by the roadside waiting for the AA to show up. It's worth getting the full bells and whistles roadside recovery cover.

To give you an idea of exactly how wrong vans can go, please indulge me briefly in a short history of some of the things we have repaired in the Beast over the last 5 years:

- Wouldn't start: Dead battery and glow plugs
- MOT Fail: All sorts of things
- Broke Down: Prop shaft snapped
- Broke Down: Disconcerting red light which indicated all-round electrical failure and caused Barny to fill up with petrol rather than diesel.
- Wouldn't start: Engine needed replacing
- MOT fail: The usual
- Health Hazzard: Smoking more than socially acceptable – timing and choke broken
- Broke Down: Engine died. Again. Another new engine.
- MOT Fail: Excessive play in the brakes
- 2nd hand engine turned out to be a rip off: Engine reconditioned.
- Unsafe to Drive: All electrics replaced
- Broke Down: Starter motor disconnected itself
- Broke Down: Fuel lines degraded
- MOT Fail: Rear suspension shot
- Listing to the right: Front suspension also gone

And that's just the big stuff. The problem is that when something is your livelihood it's hard to know when to quit. Each of these van issues cost us (on average) a few hundred pounds to repair:

Significantly less than buying a new van. Over the years we have easily spent more than the cost of another knackered old van, but we still couldn't afford a new one. This is why a big upfront investment could save you a significant pile of cash long term.

Alternatively you could look at it the other way round. What we bought is a hire-purchase Characterful Van, but we pay instalments to garages round the back of industrial estates rather than large corporate financiers. It's all just a matter of perspective.

The character element should not be ignored though. If you are selling a product that would otherwise be quite mundane, an interesting van will make it more saleable. A festival organiser will be much more likely to pick a unique van over other sellers and in a large group of gazebos a nice van will stand out. You are also much more likely to be able to secure work at weddings and private gigs, because the traditional idea of street food is focused on interesting vans. People looking for a "street food theme" will be thinking of vehicles rather than gazebos.

New vans with decent engines and sensible conversions are now also widely available. They are a great option if you want to be able to run the business solo, trading at smaller locations. A van is much more secure than a gazebo and there is no need to leave your unit while you park elsewhere. They don't have the same character of the elderly rust-buckets, but you can always add your own - and you won't need quite such a large contingency fund for when the engine drops out. A brand new conversion on a new(ish) van will cost you upwards of £10,000, so this option is not for the faint-hearted. It will mean that the only character you can add is through outside branding, which is an additional expense. Done right, you will end up with a professional-looking unit that makes your offering look more expensive and doesn't (regularly) break down on long journeys. You are much more likely to get corporate gigs (office parties etc.) with a nice new van.

I am clearly biased here, but I am not a huge fan of the commercially-converted van. Until the chains get their hands on it, street food is about soul, and a £15,000 Mercedes Sprinter conversion doesn't have a whole lot of it. Our van, the Beast, is a character in his own right. Regulars enquire after his health and wish him good luck in

MOTs. It's heart-warming. At the same time it's also expensive and a whole lot of hassle. Honestly, I don't know why we still have him.

Headroom

If you are thinking about getting a van, especially for converting yourself, then this is one point that you really must consider. We stupidly thought that stooping slightly would solve all our problems here, but unless you want a back problem before you've even started trading then you need to check you can stand up. Barny can only stand up straight in between the Beast's roof supports, can't wear high heels and still stubbornly persists at being over 6 foot.

Trading from a Trailer

I think this may be the best of both worlds. The trailer can be personalised to give it that all important character that will mean a potential customer can distinguish your unit from a burger trailer selling reheated junk. There are companies who will design and wrap your unit or you can get creative and do it yourself. You can find some amazing examples out there, and as long as it won't fall off as you cruise down the motorway at 50 mph you're fine. As with the van your kitchen is set up, ready for you to make culinary magic as soon as you're on site.

Trailers also have several advantages over vehicles:

- The much tighter turning circle means that you can navigate into a space only very slightly wider that your unit.
- During service you are actively using almost all the space available, rather than having a meter and a half of cab that sits idly waiting for you to drive away. There's a bit of tow bar, but that's it. You will really notice this when you're visiting an event that specifically requires that you pay for the frontage between yourselves and the customer.
- There are fewer things that can go wrong with a trailer. It is, after all, just a box with wheels on. Not that things don't. I've heard of rotten floors, leaky roofs, rusted chassis and blowouts on the motorway. I think there is a temptation to assume that a lack of mechanical parts mean it can't possibly go wrong. Apparently, that simply isn't true.
- Having said that, you still don't need them to pass an MOT. Your support vehicle is the only thing that needs to be reliable,

and most traders will simply use an existing car in the household until the box starts to pay for itself. Just make sure that the car in question can tow the trailer you're looking at.

On the downside you will have to tow it, which would be my personal idea of hell, because trailers appear to have a mind of their own. Check that your driving license covers you for it before you go out and buy one. You are also still wasting space, albeit less than a van, because of the gas bottle storage and tow hook. With the tide turning against the traditional festival caterers in favour of better quality offerings you may find that festivals reject you simply because it's a trailer. A lot of the application forms in recent years have been specifically looking for street fooders, and especially if your trailer starts out as a little white box they will struggle to distinguish you from the high volume/poor quality units.

Then there is also the matter of insuring it. There are people providing specialist insurance out there, and those trailers are surprisingly nickable.

Even more worryingly, recent legislation has stated that you might well need a tachograph if you are towing your vehicle with a van, 4x4 pickup or SUV[2]. Having a tacho is an extra level of complication you probably don't want to add, especially given the all-hours nature of street food. It may be worth buying a smaller van or different towing vehicle to avoid it if you can.

Gourmet from a Gazebo

With the exception of market trading, where you are using their roof and counter, the gazebo is by far the cheapest option to get started with. A simple pop-up gazebo will cost less than £100, and you are then only a few tables and a bit of window dressing away from serving that first diner. There are even benefits verses the other two options. You are, importantly, at eye level with the customers, which gives a nice feeling of equality. You also have more room than any of us trailer or van folk, because a 3m x 3m gazebo – the standard size at every event I've ever visited, gives you plenty of room to swing cats. Or cook.

---

[2] See http://www.fleetnews.co.uk/tools/tachograph/ for a tool to check compliance.

The infinite versatility of the tent means that you can also fit it into locations that are not accessible by road. This means pub beer gardens and indoor events[3] amongst others. Not only that, but as events all accept 3 metres of frontage to be the standard, you won't be paying over the odds. The Jabberwocky van needs a 6m pitch, but we only trade from a 2m hatch, effectively wasting 4m of potential selling space which we still have to pay for.

There are a few things you should know about gazebos though.

- Don't get one that assembles with poles and corners like a straw model. You need 4 people to actually get it off the ground and it will take a good half hour to build even once you know what you're doing. On a windy day this process becomes three times as hard and having thusly assembled it, it will immediately blow away.
- Pop-up gazebos, especially the cheap ones, are only a fraction more expensive, and at a pinch can be erected by one person.
- Cheap pop-up gazebos, such as those described above, are usually made of cheap metal and flimsy plastic. They will snap when you least expect them to, if they haven't blown away already.
- While we're on the subject of cheapy cheap options; They also won't be waterproof.
- In any gazebo you will get cold when it's cold. You will get wet feet when it's wet. The protection provided from the elements here is pretty basic, so while temperatures inside the van can vary by 10-15°C above what's going on outside, the gazebo will basically match the outdoor temperature.
- If it has rained and your gazebo is wet, you will need to find a way to dry your gazebo with 24 hours or it will go mouldy. Gross.
- October – April: Buy something to stand on, some solid winter boots and thermal underwear. Ideally you want a floor for the whole thing, because you just never really think about how bloody freezing the ground actually is[4].

---

[3] Trading indoors cannot involve bottled propane gas except in exceptional, carefully risk-assessed circumstances that have been signed off by a gas safe engineer. It's heavier than air, invisible and likes to blow up. Be very wary of an organiser who is happy to have gas bottles indoors.

[4] At festivals you will almost certainly need a floor, even in a support

- April – October: We van and trailer folk will start to cook gently as soon as the sun comes out. Like I said, 10-15°C above what's going on outside. In a gazebo you can just take the sides off and feel smug.

To summarize: If you really would like to make a living in street food, it's worth investing a few hundred pounds in a decent quality gazebo. For £300- £400 you can get one that is rigid enough not to turn inside-out in gentle wind and will keep the rain out. If you want to have a quick play first, just to see if street food is for you, then just make sure you get a pop-up one.

It's also worth investing in ratchet straps and cork-screw tent pegs. On a windy day your poor gazebo will be stretched to its limits, and having that go bowling away across the field (especially if you're in there cooking at the time) is no fun what so ever. We have seen them them land on us, hit our cars, collapse onto customers and just bounce joyfully away into the distance. Please make sure you tie yours down.

Van £££	Trailer ££	Gazebo £
Cold & Wind Resistant	Cold & Wind Resistant	Not as hot in Summer
Easy Setup	Easy Setup	Eye-level with customers
No support vehicle needed	Extra storage in support vehicle	More room
Fast pack up	More compact than a van	Cheap
"Characterful"	More reliable than a van	More versatile in terms of location

gazebo. A tarpaulin or rubber matting work well.

Building a Build-Up

The wild card amongst the street food setups is the build-up. You have probably seen them at German Christmas markets and occasionally at festivals. Essentially they are an extremely solid, custom-built shed, often on a solid metal frame. Like a retro van, this is your best option for ticking the "characterful" box, as you really can make these units look the part. You also benefit from the 3mx3m space bonus, just like the gazebo, but you are not going to get blown away by a gentle puff of wind, unlike many of your gazebo-based buddies.

The downside to these setups is, unfortunately, the setup. While a team of two can get a gazebo up (and importantly, waterproof) in less than 30 seconds it will take time to assemble a build-up. The components are heavy, everything has to be unloaded and carried and reassembled and later disassembled and carried and packed away. To put it in perspective, we can arrive and be serving 15 minutes later if we want to, 30 minutes if we're dawdling or one of us wanders off for a chat. Our build-up buddies arrive 1.5 to 2 hours before an event. I would probably recommend this for pro users, or folks who really love a challenge.

Mid January 2011

We had successfully bought a van. It was in Romford, London, which wasn't ideal, and had no MOT, which should probably have been a clue. On the other hand, it was now ours, meaning we had somehow begun a street food business, although we didn't really know it yet. We trundled down to my parent's house, collected my dad and older brother, and headed for London.

Money changed hands, pieces of paper moved in various directions, keys were explained, as were buttons, methods to kicking the back door at the right angle to pop off the padlock and long wheel base driving. It struck me that long wheel base driving looked much, much longer than it had on the pictures.

Barny would be driving. My dad and brother, originally invited along to kick tyres and make disapproving noises on our behalf (neither myself nor Barny knew much about cars in those days), took the 4×4 and we narrowly missed a tree on the way to the main road.

The main road itself was an abundance of traffic. The van didn't mind. It was not going to hurry. The power that you would expect from a motorised vehicle was absent. Despite a huge amount of noise, making it sound like the engine was moments away from exploding, there was very little to show for it. We did our best to swear at it; universally accepted time-honoured way to make any car go faster, but 30 miles an hour was apparently quite enough. This would effectively rule out motorway travel, which meant arriving back in Leamington some time tomorrow.

Spirits dampened we considered things, stopped for petrol and then decided that we would either have to ignore the pitiful scream of pain coming from the engine or accept defeat at the very first hurdle. We floored the van, cringing as the sound of a thousand tiny rabbits roared in pained unison. A brief stint of downhill, and the van cleared 40 miles per hour.

Concerns abandoned we gunned slowly for the motorway, with the engine continuing its crazed bunny lament and a mildly embarrassed 4×4 pottering along ahead of us. The slip road was steep, we crawled up it, fairly sure that 20 miles an hour was too slow for 3 lanes of traffic. Then gravity came to our rescue. We caught up with my dad's 4×4, waved and gesticulated frantically (poss. some swearing – unconfirmed) and they got the message and sped up. 56 miles per hour; we finally had speed.

The van made the rest of the journey without incident, even when we stopped to pick up our car from my parent's house and continued onwards up the M40. It was a pained smoky start from their house, but a start nonetheless. We drove back to our old flat and carefully parked the van in the car park outside our lower ground floor flat, reasoning that here it would be most out of everyone's way.

It blocked the entire front room window, giving everything an odd yellow hue that would have otherwise been ominously sickly. I thought it was nice; knowing that the van, at that time our most valuable possession, was safe right outside the window.

It dominated the car park, towering over lesser vehicles around it in determined silence. We were delighted. The two lads selling the van were quitting the mobile catering industry entirely, having realised that it was going nowhere and would never make them any money. This meant that along with the vehicle itself we had also inherited several hundred pounds worth of catering paraphernalia, some of which we are still using four years later.

Despite the January weather, which was bitterly cold in 2011, we turned out the van into our living room, delightedly uncovering one thing after another and cataloguing it for prosperity (and later our accountant). Notable finds included several hundred ordering pads, which we still use for inevitable "let me write that down somewhere" moments, 23 surprisingly short aprons, the longest of which have been very handy and a full size, extremely solid A-Board, which is something of a street food must-have.

A Note About A-Boards

A good street food market is characterised by a high volume of A-boards. So much so that some locations will restrict the use of space in front of your stall; otherwise the venue becomes a slalom race between and around the boards. At a market when all the stalls are laid out in rows, the A-board serves as a way of diverting attention to your product, pointing their forward gaze to where you are standing on the left or right. You need to make sure that they look at your board and then look at you, so choose your words wisely.

Awards are excellent content. If you do manage to win one, get it on that board. It makes your food more valuable and therefore instantly better value for money. We won an award in the middle of 2013, but people only knew about it once it was on the board. In the absence of an award, state your product, with a price if you have a nice simple menu. In the competitive world of securing the customer's next meal, you need to speak to stomach and pocket alike.

We also use our board as a prop. It advised that in eating street food – specifically our street food – they were "Sticking it to the man". Delighted groups of teenagers would occasionally take pictures of themselves ironically striking poses next to it. Teenagers aren't really going to buy our food, preferring the flabby burger, but photo opportunities, especially in this social media world, are not to be sniffed at.

There are many other things you can coat it with, use your imagination on that one. How well sourced your ingredients are or your local credentials, feedback from customers and menus or specials are all a good call. Then you just have to decide where to place it, which does have a little more art to it than you might think.

If you are in a restricted space with very heavy crowds then put the board at one end of your stall, right in close. It then forms a flood barrier that will stop potential customers being swept away with the crowds. If you are in a wider space put in front and centre, a good few meters away. It will then funnel people towards your unit as they read the board. If you get unlucky and get a rubbish pitch then whip out your pens, add a big old arrow and put it in the footfall, within sight of your stall. Just be aware that most of your pitches will need to be accessible to fire engines in an emergency and organisers might need to move your board if it's in an escape route. Try not to put it in front of anyone else's stall either, that's just bad form.

After a year of labour on the van and plans to ultimately franchise the canary-coloured monster as "the yellow van co" and get rich the two lads who converted it had grown bored. They realised that their passion was for converting, not for street food. From the remains of the van's kitchen; at that point scattered round our living room, we concluded that although they were registered as a falafel van they had actually been selling tinned hot dogs and packet noodles.

If it weren't for the appalling food they would have been one of the first real street food vans in London, possibly a member of the London street food elite by now, but it worked out well for us. As we emptied out tin after slightly rusty tin of hotdogs we began to realise that we too, were going to need to decide what to sell.

Deciding What to Sell

While following your dream is a worthy cause, that dream still needs to pay the rent. Assuming you don't have unlimited resources then the food you choose needs to tick all the following points:

1. It has to make you money
2. You need to be able to cook it
3. Other people have to want to buy it
4. The serving time has to be fast
5. You have to like it yourself

Here are the other differences that you need to consider when picking your food type.

Prep Time Vs. Service Time

As a general rule, the more time you invest before the event, the faster it is to serve on the day. Unlike all other toastie sellers I've met, we prepare our sandwiches in advance, and then cook them to order. It means out total time spent on each order during service is around 20 seconds (we take more orders while the toastie is cooking) rather than 2-4 minutes. It means we can serve hundreds of toasties an hour, rather than one every 2-4 minutes. But we send hours the day before painstakingly building toasties.

Burgers have to be cooked and assembled to order, but involve very little up front prep. Pulled pork, on the other hand, has to be smoked, pulled and stored before the event, but just needs to be dropped in the bun on the night.

Ingredients

Ingredients will probably surprise you. As a consumer, we largely regard food, especially restaurant food, as being basically free. Money-grubbing restaurateurs are just out for a fast buck. This is mostly not true. Especially at the street food end of the spectrum you will want to use good quality ingredients, because that's how you get the reputation for greatness. Good ingredients, even when bought in bulk, still cost actual money.

Popularity

It is commonly thought that, the quality being equal, all foods will sell at the same approximate rate. It's not true, there is a hierarchy, and knowing it can help you make a better choice. Here are your top street food groups, sorted in approximate order of desirability by customers, although this will change depending on location and crowd affluence and attitude.

I'll rate each on ingredients and Prep time verses service time as well, just to give you an idea.

Burgers
Service time heavy. High ingredient costs.

Between you and me, burgers sell best. Almost every time. My personal, cynical theory is that we have all been brainwashed by McWorldDomination due to years of exposure to their advertising, but the fact remains that even a bad burger will often outsell everything else two to one. By bad I mean that it can be a cheap, limp, barely meat patty of wafer thinness in a bun that has only a passing resemblance to bread with a slice of orange-yellow plastic; *it will still outsell you*.

Before you chuck it all in and invest in a white trailer and a pallet full of horse burgers there is a silver lining. Most of those customers will only buy a burger from there once. These guys do not rely on repeat custom; they rely on having an attractive price-point to those who are short on cash and low on food. As street food spreads, festival organisers, tired of hearing that their food offerings are worse than prisons and NHS wards, are starting to actively search for a quality product.

Offer a delicious burger and you are potentially sitting on a meaty little gold mine. In Birmingham there are several burger sellers who score top of the desirability lottery and have managed to successfully carve out an entirely deserved reputation as one of the finest burgers in town, arguably the finest. Their reputation and beautifully managed campaign of never quite bringing enough mean that they hold the perfect position as *the* must-try food on the Brum street food scene. No other foodstuff can match the burger for desirability amongst punters.

Choosing to serve burgers might therefore seem like a sound financial investment and a great way to win street food.

The downside is that you are one of a multitude. While serving the best burger in town will quite possibly make you a local hero in the eyes of your customers, it also means that you will never get a spot at a festival. You will be up against literally hundreds of other folks, gourmet burgering like their lives depend on it. There will be pickles and homemade 'slaw everywhere. So: great for local trade at farmers markets, street food events and private functions, but not for the big money weekenders unless you have connection who can get you in.

Pulled Pork
Prep Time Heavy, Medium-High ingredient costs.

This is the new, up and coming street food rude boy. Inspired by the BBQ competitions of the USA, you take a hunk of meat, usually pork, and smoke it. Serve much like the gourmet burger with your relishes and slaw and brioche buns.

This is a very street food option; managing to be both wildly mainstream and hipster-pleasing all in one go. There is a lot of work involved in doing it properly, as you will need a commercial smoker and a lot of free time to feed that smoker with wood chips and meat. It is a great example of the classic catering conundrum: The more prep you do in advance, the faster your service will be. Smoked, slow cooked meats are incredibly time-consuming to prepare (smoke it, pull it down, store it), but only have to be reheated on the day and they're ready to serve.

However you have a careful balancing act of heating up pork, using pork and being left with pork at the end. Once you have reheated that meat it has to get sold, otherwise it's going in the bin at the end of the day.

Sausages & Hog Roasts
Heavy prep time if you are doing it street food style. Otherwise light prep and service time. Medium-high ingredient costs.

In many cases, these traders pre-date the street food industry by years, but are happy to be included on the bandwagon if it's heading their way. Often they are farmers or butchers who have expanded into market or festival catering, alongside selling their produce. These options are, for most customers, the best thing that isn't a burger. In certain places they will even outsell burgers, notably a nice visible hog roast at any festival with a medieval feel to it or a Bratwurst at a German Christmas market.

The hog roast is a long established staple of the British market scene, and although they do have excellent theatre in the process: Spit-roasting a pig does look impressive; on its own this does not really count as street food. Usually this is because it is served in a processed bun, with wholesale apple sauce and Paxo stuffing.

Sausage in a bun, similarly, is a familiar sight at markets. Often these are local farm sausages and the bun could well be locally baked, so these folks would count under my personal definition of street food. Usually it is just a straight up sausage with some onions and mustard, so anything different would be an interesting change and a selling point when applying for pitches. You will find, though, that markets are often closed to you. The sausage sellers and hog roasters trading there will have been doing so for donkey's years, and you will probably struggle to even get a response from the market organisers. Festivals, similarly, will already have someone doing sausage, and may not be able to distinguish between your amazing, knock-your-socks-off sausage and one straight from the freezer.

Fish & Chips
High prep time if you are doing it street food style. Otherwise light prep and service time. Medium-high ingredient costs.

This is another classic outdoor dish that has undergone a street food revival, and now reaps the rewards. Apart from being one of the few vendors who can do chips, which sell everywhere, all the time, you also serve a British classic that holds a very special place in everyone's hearts.

As people don't really like their classic to be messed with there is not much you can change about this without potentially losing custom, but be brave. Everyone knows a really good chippy, and if you are that chippy word will spread. To actually make this a street food concept rather than a basic chip van consider serving interesting, freshly caught fish, making your own chips and battering the unbatterable.

On the down side, due to the amount of oil involved it will be very hard to run from a gazebo, meaning that in summer you will be standing in your sweaty little van or trailer with half a dozen fryers pumping out heat in excess of 100°C. You will boil. You will also be paying through the nose for all that electricity. Add to that the ever-fluctuating price of fish and probably the highest setup costs in street food: fryers, hot-holding displays, chipper, rumbler and some way of keeping all that food cold. It's not quite as easy as it might seem

World Food
High prep time; low service time. Medium to low ingredient costs.

This delightfully broad spectrum covers everything that isn't European or American. Thai, Indian, Chinese, Peruvian, Malaysian, Mexican, South African –in competition terms, this all falls into much the same bracket. Considering the number of Chinese and Indian takeaways in most towns it's surprising that there aren't more street food vendors selling amazing international cuisine, but at the moment they are still reasonably rare outside London.

There are quite a few festival caterers specialising in (often simplified or generic) versions of cuisines from around the world (Noodles! Curry!), so you may still struggle to get into the big summer gigs, but at street food markets you should be onto a winner. Dedicated street food markets are where people want to experiment with food, so give them regional specialities and delicacies, but consider having a more recognisable option or ingredient on the menu for generic events and emerging foodies.

You will probably do quite well on private bookings if you have a good looking unit, but will struggle to secure public bookings where you are the only caterer there – organisers tend towards the safe, something-for-everyone option.

As with the vegan and veggie food sellers, you should be able to negotiate on fees at bigger events because you will be the only applicant selling your type of food, so make sure you ask. It's rare

44

that you will lose a pitch because of it, and you might end up saving a few hundred pounds.

Sweets
Low-medium prep time; medium service time. Low ingredient costs.

The heavyweights here are pancakes (crepes) and churros. These are, in the dessert world, the equivalent of the burger. This means that no matter how bad that pancake is, it will outsell a more obscure dessert easily. If you are considering sweets there are lots to choose from, but very few events will have room for more than one or two sweet caterers, no matter how exciting the food appears.

On the other hand your ingredient costs will be significantly lower, as the main components will probably be flour, milk, eggs and sugar in some combination. You can still charge street food sort of prices though, so while you might sell fewer (around half as many perhaps), your profits will be higher. Negotiate with organisers, emphasising your locally sourced produce and freshly made batter and you might be able to festival yourself happy.

A word of warning: at busy festivals you will need to bring your own food or get friendly with your neighbours fast. Living off nothing but churros will break your spirit. We (the savoury vendors) are normally more than happy to go for swaps, though.

Giant Frying Pan Food
Prepped entirely on site, but cannot be sold until cooked. Fast service. Medium ingredient costs.

Paella, jambalaya, chilli and wraps – the name is a give-away. This food is as much about the theatre as it is about the taste. Great big pans of colourful meat, veg and rice, steaming away right there in front of you are intoxicatingly tempting. Along with that you are serving something that most people are familiar with but would not necessarily cook at home, so treating themselves while on the go, especially when it looks as good as that, is perfectly justified.

The biggest downside here is probably the wastage. This is because you are hot-holding. You cook it, and then keep it above 63 degrees until you serve it (although there are exceptions, this is the safest way to think – get it wrong and people can get seriously ill). To hold everything in a large, open, flat pan at 63 degrees you will need more than 63degrees of heat, so most things will continue to cook, meaning that a batch of cooked paella, which starts the day tasting great, will not taste nearly as good by the end of lunch. You need fast and furious sales for the food to work properly, and at the end of the day anything you have left will have to go in the bin.

Getting the timings right is also going to be a pain, because you might start lunch with a huge queue, hopefully put on a second batch of paella and then all those customers evaporate for no reason and your paella goes in the bin. It's a matter of practise, and you will get a feel for repeat events after a while. The wastage will be painful, but thankfully your main ingredient is generally rice, which is not nearly as costly as throwing out large quantities of meat.

Giant frying pan food is a great, visual addition to busy markets. If you can work a big festival you should get into those as well, especially if you have a nice setup.

Cheese-based Food
High service time (generally speaking). Low (pizza, jackets) – high (toasties, raclette) ingredient costs.

Pizza, toasties, jacket potatoes and raclette are totally different beasts, but it's very hard to sell someone two cheese-based foods in the same day. We, as toastie people, try not to end up too close to the pizza, because in the grand scheme of things people find pizza more desirable than toasties. Cheese-related products are familiar but a little less desirable than meat-in-a-bun, but we can have more variation than almost any other food. We straddle both vegetarian and meat customers, we're effortlessly familiar and so are able to trade alone.

This means that at small events where only one trader is needed we can fill the gap, while a burger or hotdog vendor would not cater for the veggies unless they brought a second grill. With vegetarians though, you should be aware that unless to have an entirely separate pizza oven or toastie press your food is not technically vegetarian. Making claims to the contrary could get you into trouble with trading

46

standards. We don't claim any of our food is vegetarian, but if asked what is suitable we explain which toasties contain no meat, and everything is cooked on the same press. We can always wrap toasties in tin foil is separate cooking is required.

Due to the variation in our foods we will potentially get more morning trade than our compatriots and can act as a snack or a main meal, but when the lunch queues form, it's the burger queue you will be watching, every single time.

Sandwiches & Subs

Low prep time, high service time. Medium-high ingredient costs.

This is very close to both burgers and toasties, but can probably just about warrant its own category. If only to warn you that **cold sandwiches will not sell**. Whatever you put in that roll, it needs to be hot, it needs to be filthy (think CIABTT – Can I Add Bacon To That) and it needs to sound delicious in writing.

You will probably be looking at something like meatballs, cooked fresh and then melted in a bun with cheese, or philly cheese steak, or something similar. They're all good filthy options, and if you can manage to cook them in a visual way (flambé!) they will also sell well. Just don't set anyone on fire. You will have most of the same problems as the burger sellers, but with a lower overall appeal.

Vegetarian

Prep time and service time medium, ingredient cost low-medium.

Depending on who you ask, the veggie population is somewhere between 5 and 10%. That percentile is going to be 90% of your custom. Most meat-eaters will automatically rule you out. Sorry.

Whether it's falafel, pakoras, wraps, soup, salads or curries, as a purely veggie and/or vegan vendor you will find a unique set of challenges. I'll be honest with you; you are hoping to sell the least desirable of the mainstream street foods. More than anyone else, at markets you will be watching people queue at other stalls.

But that's markets. At large street food events you will have a monopoly on the vegetarians and at festivals, assuming that your food is delicious - as I imagine it would be - you will find that the ratio of vegetarians spikes in your favour. I'm not sure whether it's because there are actually more veggies at festivals or whether they just eat more veggie food because of the general sense of oneness with nature when you're sleeping in a muddy field, but it seems to sell better.

Added bonus: you have more negotiation capabilities because people want to have you there. You are a rarity, and as an organiser they don't have to work out if vegetarian options are covered. I would probably recommend that you do veggie and vegan rather than just veggie – as a festival organiser you will tick more boxes for them, making you a more appealing choice.

Pasta
Done street food style: High service time, medium prep time. Med-Low ingredient costs.

I've seen quite a few people doing this, often using dried pasta and ready-made sauces. I think you are setting yourself quite a challenge. The main reason people buy street food is because they couldn't do it themselves. A vast majority of us know the theory of making a burger, but we choose not to. We can slow roast a shoulder of pork for 12 hours and then put it in a bun, but we don't have the time. We can buy a frozen pizza, but everyone knows it tastes better fresh.

Pasta and sauce, however, is something that almost everyone can cook, even if they are using Dolmio. If you do decide to make a living out of pasta, you need to find a way to make it sexy. Make your own pasta on site, cook your sauces in a giant frying pan and buy one of those enormous pepper mills. Dried pasta and a bottled sauce isn't street food, but done properly pasta can be.

Everything Else
If you have an idea for something else not mentioned above then you deserve a small round of applause. The brand new ideas are the ones that all the street food events and collectives are looking for,

and they will welcome you with open arms. Events in general will be falling over themselves to have you on board.

But there is always a down side to these things. While at street food events you will do reasonably well, at larger festivals you may find that your food is just too strange. In our experience people want something familiar, but cooked in an interesting way. If you can't explain your food in 3 words then people won't understand enough to part with money.

Times are changing, and in London you can sell some delightfully obscure stuff these days, but out here - beyond the M25 - you may struggle initially. I *would* say stick with it, ride the storm and weather the losses, but it's a business, and not making money sucks. I'd rather you made money.

Don't bin that great idea though. If you are passionate enough to make it work then it will happen. Pick your events carefully, try and have something familiar enough that customers don't have to ask for details, somewhere on your menu, so that you have a wide enough appeal to make money. Make sure your unit looks the part. There are lots of people out there pushing the boundaries; you could be one of them. Find that perfect food that hits the popular hipster appeal just right and you could really make a name for yourself.

Hot Drinks

There are two distinct types of hot drink, which have very different markets. The first can be used to compliment your product. Any of the above businesses will lend themselves to adding a tea urn and then selling instant coffee and tea-bag tea. It means keeping your boiler hot, bringing cups, sugar, stirrers, milk and a bin. That's about it. If you can co-ordinate this alongside your existing service then you will add a small but significant revenue stream, because hot drinks are almost entirely profit.

Then there are the espresso drinks, which are almost exclusively provided by a dedicated seller. If you do choose this route you are looking at low turnover, but high profit margins. People will happily pay several pounds for a proper latte, cappuccino or otherwise frothed milk beverage, and you can always add cakes and snacks for extra sales goodness.

This does work out at a lot of time for a comparatively small amount of turnover. While the hot food traders will be earning hundreds of pounds an hour with a queue, you will be limited by how fast you can make a latte, and although it might take as long as the hot food per portion, you still can't charge anywhere like as much.

February 2011

Decisions were failing us. We needed to find food with theatre, something delicious (obviously), something different but familiar and something that would make us money. We wanted to do something that had never been done out on the street, because with a name like the Jabberwocky we had a lot to live up to.

Meanwhile, in the real world, we needed an MOT.

We had secured the Beast for our original budget because he had no MOT. We were assured that he still ran, and that there was no reason for him to fail one, the previous owners simply hadn't managed to book it. Or so we were told. My goodness we can be gullible when we want something.

We had the van booked in for his MOT a few days after collection, and the plan was to start applying for events and taking positive, life-affirming steps directly after that. The only problem was that he wouldn't start. A few days before that he had been just fine, we'd driven him all the way back from London without incident, and now he appeared to be dead.

We rebooked the appointment for another day, and apologized to our garage. A few hours later we just about had him, jumpstarting him off our other car, but you can hardly expect your garage to wheel spare vehicles in every time it does start just so they can MOT your heap of junk.

After the third missed test they asked us to make sure it started before we booked it in again.

This left us in a tricky position. We couldn't start it because it didn't start. No one would come and see it because it was a knackered old van that looked a lot more effort that it was worth. It is, quite simply, much easier to take a problem to someone who can fix it than to rely on the fixer coming out to you. We spoke to 3 different mobile mechanics: every single one in the area. They all made reassuring promises to come and fix things on a particular date and time. None of them ever turned up.

For this reason, by the end of February, we were beginning to get a bit frantic. We had hoped to already be at least road-legal by then. Our very expensive hobby was only 6 weeks old at that point and was literally going nowhere.

Instead we decided to work on the type of food we actually wanted to sell. Previous ideas had included "balls of stuff" served in a cone. Our plan was to take food, make it into balls, cook and serve it. It sat on the drawing board for a while, but although service would be a doddle, there seemed to be very few foods that would benefit, taste-wise, from being "balled".

Instead we concentrated on Barny's speciality, which is modern British cuisine. We thought that miniature versions of classic British flavour combinations would surely tick all the boxes we had identified as being important: Needs to be tasty, needs to be original and exciting, needs to make us money.

Our next step was to test our food on friends to see if it was actually as good as we thought. We invited as many of our friends as we had chairs for, and Barny spent the day studiously using every kitchen utensil we owned while I tried to stay ahead of the washing up. The plan was to exchange free food for challenging and thoughtful criticism, by means of the ever-trusted survey sheet.

We were still trying to work the balls-of-things concept, but had morphed it into this idea of having bite-size chunks of everything, to allow for sharing and thus hopefully encourage people to actually try it. On the menu that night, all served in one of several thousand Styrofoam cups we had acquired with the van, were:
- Meatballs
- Carrot fritters

- Garlic mushrooms
- Scampi
- Dough balls
- Savoury profiteroles
- Banana fritters
- Brownie chunks

I was mostly too nervous to actually try anything, but later, as we talked things over with quite a lot of sloe gin it became clear that the concept, whilst generally enjoyed, is difficult to explain in one sentence. I kept finding myself using phrases like "similar to" and "sort of like". It felt wrong that I should trying to convince an eager public that this amazing concept is sort of like a burger van but classier, or similar to one of those vegetarian independent vans but without the hemp.

Our original idea of "balls of food" whilst being unique, was almost impossible to explain without it sounding like an incomplete innuendo. Our restaurant style food, on the other hand, got a better reception and, although it still needed a fair bit of tweaking, could be explained without putting you off your dinner.

Tasting Nights and Surveys

We reckon to have friends over at least once a year to try our food. It's a good excuse for an interesting night in, and now that most of our mates are survey night veterans they are happy to tell us when they don't like something. It also means that when we disagree on a toastie, or are not great fans of them in the first place, we can get the results independently verified.

Make sure you order the food on the sheet in the same order that it comes out of the kitchen. Once a few gins had been downed I'm pretty sure half the scores were in the wrong places.

Regular tasting sessions have provided us with excellent feedback for all stages of our menu. We make it as scorable as possible, so use numbers rather than getting people to write long passages about feelings. It means you can tot things up and compare at the end, which ultimately leaves you with much more useful data than the thoughtful but tipsy ramblings of your best bud.

Plus it makes a memorable night out amongst friends, and reminds us that we have a social circle outside the walls of the van.

Late February 2011

The food was decided, but the van was still earnestly clogging up our driveway. We were, despite my superficially cheery attitude in blog posts at the time; the proud owners of something that would do nothing more than make us a few hundred pounds in scrap metal.

I was determined to maintain my optimism though, and began trying to work out how we could make our project into a business. The data available online on this subject is vast, but after days of searching we found it surprisingly easy to set up a limited company online.

Choosing a Legal structure

There are 3 main structures you can choose from when you're starting a street food business. Depending on your structure you will have different levels of responsibility regarding your paperwork. There are many, many forms of company around, but you will need one of the following three forms, unless you are an accountancy wiz or tax evasion specialist.

I'll cover the points that are significant to our industry, but I'm not an accountant, so if you know one then please talk to them. They will be able to give you much better guidance, based on your specific situation.

Sole trader

You are the company, the company is you and any money the company makes is yours, subject to taxation and whatnot. If you are a one man or woman band, this is your best bet. You are self-employed, so at the end of the year you do your self-assessment and pay your taxes. Bear in mind that you have to pay taxes later, not at

...it of earing, like with a regular job. Money you take is not
...atically yours: you have to give some of it back later. Bummer.

Another note-worthy downside: if somebody sues your company,
they are also suing you. This means all your assets (house, car, TV)
are technically also part of the business. If the company gets into
debt for any reason, you may have to sell your house to pay it off.

Contrary to popular belief you can still have employees as a sole
trader. You will need to run payroll, just like any other company.
Paperwork-tastic.

Partnership

Sole trading for two: Two people who are both responsible for the
company financially and agree to certain terms and responsibilities
within a company. Make sure, even if you're a couple or BFFs, that
you put down in writing how you want this relationship to work. Talk
about problems early, before they become issues, and try to stay
friends. Again this is a low-paperwork option, perfect for two people
who don't have any major assets.

Limited Company

To the general public, this option makes you look like a proper,
legitimate business. Weirdly, it actually absolves you of far more
financial responsibility than the others, but it saddles you with a
mountain of paperwork to compensate and much more expensive
accountancy.

"Limited" refers to your level of responsibility should the worst
happen. The company is a separate legal entity, and you cannot be
held responsible for its actions (financially, that is. Go on a killing
spree with company property and I'm sure the tax office would
manage to hold you liable for the clean-up). Think of it as an extra
person. You, the directors, are responsible for deciding exactly what
this person does, where is does it and why. The assumption is that
you have the best interests of your darling company at heart, and
would never do anything to harm it.

Just supposing you did though, the only assets that can be used to
pay off any resulting debt are ones belonging to the company: Your
unit, your cooking equipment and your fluffy rear-view mirror dice.

54

Your house has nothing to do with it, assuming you have not spent company money on installing a swanky prep kitchen.

By the way: Festival organisers are well aware of limited company magic as well. They start a company, take your cash and put on an event so staggeringly bad that you are almost more impressed than angry. Before you know it the have declared bankruptcy and disappeared like a bad smell in a high wind. Big, one-off sporting events are often blighted with this. Watch yourself.

Choosing

Your circumstances will dictate the best structure to go for. If you are unsure and don't have anyone to ask, you may want to go for being a sole trader. You can always change to a limited company later, and this is (assuming nothing goes wrong) the cheaper option.

There is a lot of specialist advice out there and, between you and me; there are a fair few grants and loans out there for people starting out in their first year of business. They vary regionally, so you will have to do your research on what's available near you.

I would strongly recommend seeking advice from someone who has set up a business before. Not so that you can copy their methods, but so that you can ask them the little questions that will irk you in the middle of the night otherwise. The legal obligations, especially of a limited company, usually end with a fine, so you need to be on the ball. You have to start opening and taking notice of daunting brown envelopes when they come through the door. If you are the kind of person who likes to file bills in the bin until they cut you off, please don't go for a limited company unless you have a good accountant on board and they are your registered address.

Late February 2011

We set up a limited company. We wanted something future-proof that wouldn't risk any future houses we might buy, and where we could both give ourselves job titles like "Director".

With the company came certain responsibilities, notably things like HMRC taking a sudden interest in you and the occasional email from Companies House threatening you with large fines if you don't keep your details up to date. The first few official pieces of correspondence were quite worrying, but that's just how they talk to everyone, and they really don't mean it like that.

Setting up the company was a big step though, and we felt it was only right to stop being downhearted about the failing rust-bucket in the car park and take some positive steps. These positive steps were the ones we should have taken right from the start, which was to get my brother and dad round again. The folks who originally helped us buy the van were the same ones who finally got it working in our hour of need, where everyone else had failed us. It needed new glow plugs, new wiring and a new battery. After a day of working out what the problem might be and a mad dash to get to Halfords before closing time there was a moment of truth. With a cloud of dramatic smoke and a roar that shook the prim Leamington street, the van finally roared into life.

Since then there have only been seven or eight occasions when I have been as pleased as that to hear a vehicle start. In every case it has been the Beast. Characterful vans have that about them.

With the van alive and well our next step was to start getting him legal, so that we could actually trade. Before that we had decided to tell the landlord about our business and make sure he was fine with us using the flat as a base for operations. He wasn't.

Although you are normally allowed to run businesses from home, there are certain statutes and clauses that mean if you rent, your landlord can get upset about you running a business. In the long term this turns out to have been a good thing, because it was what finally made us decide to buy our own house, which turned out to be cheaper than renting anyway. This was 2011, right after house prices had completed their credit-crunch nose-dive. Technically there can also be sections written into your property deeds that mean you can't run a business even when you own the house, but unless you give

56

someone cause to complain, this should never become an issue.

Buying a house took up most of our free time in March and April that year, meaning that street food progress was slow and, although we didn't know it, we were already missing the applications window for summer events.

Applying for One-Off Events

Events that only take place once a year are usually organised by a dedicated group of people, whether they are the local council, the local BID (Business Improvement District – they work to promote the town and therefore being more people to the centre), a group of enthusiasts or a company, they all try and get the catering ticked off nice and early.

This is because your fees from the catering concessions are often what pays for the rest of the festival, so they want to have you booked in well before the line-up is announced, usually in the first three months of the New Year, so that your fees can be used to pay for the acts. When we first started out most street food events were these one-off food- or music festivals, as outside London street food didn't really exist. Now you can find dedicated street food markets popping up across the country, so don't panic if you are starting after March – the big events are stupidly expensive and a huge financial risk. In your first year you are probably better off staying small and refining your product and procedures, especially if you are still working full time.

If you want to tackle the big events then start with the earliest one and work your way forwards through the year. Don't apply more than a year in advance, because they won't even consider you until the current festival is out the way and everyone has had a few weeks to recover. Then you can send them an email to ask to be included in the mailing list – and from December onwards you should start finding updated information on the application process for the following year on their website. I'll go into more detail on the exact application process later.

March 2011

It was time to try and make the van, now generally known as the Beast, a legal and functioning method for serving food. We were still buying a house, and while that was taking place we were finally getting the van MOTed, taxed and officially registered in our name. At the same time there were a bunch of legal obligations that needed to be covered to be allowed to trade. Currently the law is changing in our favour on that one, but it means we need to be more careful than ever before to make sure we're safe.

Health & Safety

There are a few big parts to registering a food business once you have your company. They can happen in any order, but they all need to be in place before you can trade at any events.

Create a folder on your computer called "health and safety stuff" and put an electronic copy of each document in there as it comes through. Save it as [your business][document name][expiry date] for added ease (Jabberwocky Public Liability July 2016, for example). Buy a document wallet and print out a hard copy, file them in there and take that with you each time you trade. Update both each time a document expires and archive the old version. Event organisers hate having to chase you for documents, so being able to pre-empt that is a huge selling point and will mean they remember you fondly. It also means that applications become dreamy, simple exercises where you simply fire a bunch of collated paperwork off into the internet.

You may want to invest in a scanner, but a photo, as long as it is legible, should work just as well. Being as you will need to do a ton of printing it is probably worth having the company invest in a scanner/printer combo. It will make life easier. These are the things you will be asked for. Not all of them every time, but over the course of the year you will probably need all of them at some stage, and many will come up every time.

1. Register your food business with the local council
2. Get Food Hygiene Certificates

3. A Gas Safe test
4. A PAT (Portable Appliance Test) Certificate
5. Public, Employers' and Product Liability Insurance
6. Risk Assessment
7. HACCPs
8. Cleaning Rota & Temperature Records
9. Method Statement
10. Have your business inspected and rated by the EHO

1. *Registering a Food Business*

You need to know what council you are living in, and you need a computer. Gather together the details you were sent when you set up the company, and make yourself a brew. Bring up a search engine of your choice and type "registering a food business [your district council]". In our case I'd type "registering a food business Warwick district council" and as if by magic I'm whisked to the right form.

Local councils all have slightly different infrastructure, so don't be too worried if it isn't the top hit, it will be in there somewhere. If all else fails, ring the council, they will be able to point you in the right direction.

At this stage you are not specifically starting a *street food* business. There is another form out there that might crop up in your searches, the "street trading license", which is totally different and you can thankfully ignore at the moment. This is for your permanent pitch, if you eventually choose to try for one. At this stage I would avoid it unless you have a clear business plan and know a great pitch with excellent footfall. Get yourself set up, legal and making money first.

The form for registering your business is very straight forward if you have the details to hand. All you're doing is informing the council of what's going on, so they can set the wheels in motion for getting an inspection for you from the Environmental Health. As this is a registration rather than a license it shouldn't get turned down, but you do need to do it at least a month before you want to start to trade. I would get onto it as soon as you have your company, as it is free to do and only takes a few minutes.

The confirmation of registration is a letter that doesn't look like anything much, and can easily get buried in the paperwork graveyard. You won't often get asked for this, but occasionally festival organisers want to see it. This is the first of your health & safety collection.

2. *Get a Food Hygiene Certificate*

Before the Environmental Health come round for the first time you need to be certified to handle food. This is the only formal qualification you need. It costs around £30 and can be done in 3 hours online. It teaches you the basics about food handling and cleaning, and is all reasonably straight forward. Most of the courses offer unlimited free retakes and will then post the certificate straight to you.

There are three levels, but as a cook you will want level two, and be planning to do level three at some stage in the future. Scan the certificate once you have it. It goes in the file.

3. *Gas Safety Test*

You only need this if you have gas appliances. If you trade from a gazebo then you will be looking at one single gas appliance (like a grill) connected to one single gas bottle. This means only that appliance needs to be inspected, which is significantly cheaper than the van/trailer alternative. A brand new appliance comes with a gas safety test for the first year, all others, including refurbished second hand ones, should be taken to a gas safety technician and certified.

The rules for vans are stricter: your gas work has to be solid pipes rather than flexible hoses (except 1m directly from bottle to initial pipework) and the unit will need ventilation. Overall, you will probably end up spending at least a few hundred pounds on the work if there wasn't anything in place to begin with. New installations will also need extraction, which can cost significantly more.

4. *PAT Certificate*

A PAT certificate is only necessary if you have mains electric appliances, so if you run your setup off batteries then you don't need to worry about it. If you will require mains power, try and keep it to a minimum. Make sure you know how much power you draw, both in amps and kilowatts. This will come up in application forms all the time, and putting in the wrong amount will either mean you are the inconsiderate moron tripping the power for everyone else, or you're the generous soul who spent way too much on power. The PAT guy is a good person to ask if you have no idea, or try searching the exact make and model of the appliance.

You may also think that if you have a gas or BBQ setup there is no need for any form of electrics. It's a noble thought, but eventually you're going to have to accept that it gets dark.

While you may be able to operate using sonar, which is a nifty trick, granted, there is another problem: Customers want to see you. In the grand scheme of things lights are not there for you to see by – chances are you could use the torch on your phone if you really got in a pickle; they are so that you can be seen. A bright, inviting unit will easily steal sales off the folks trading in the dark nearby.

5. *Public Liability Insurance*
Like any other insurance, you should compare prices. You will need £5,000,000 minimum of Public and Product, 10 million of Employers, but this is usually the standard amount, and it should all be in one policy.

While the numbers sound scary, the actual policy will probably be between 100 and 200 pounds. You will almost certainly never have to use it, but it's there as a safety net for you and the general public.

You will need an idea of your anticipated turnover (don't aim for the stars here, that will put the price up – be realistic) what you will be serving from and a few details about your company.

When anticipating turnover it's worth knowing that earning more than the current VAT threshold will mean you have to pay VAT. This means giving 20% of everything you ear to the VAT man. More on that later, but I wouldn't expect your turnover to be anywhere beyond that in your first year, lower if you are not financially reliant on the business. See VAT in chapter 6 for more.

PLI is the document you will most frequently be asked for. An organiser's top priority is knowing that you are insured so that if you screw up, they won't have to take the fall.

6. Risk Assessment

You will need to actually create this document, but there are loads of templates you can use online. The aim here is to consider your unit as nothing short of a murderous death trap, and then try and find ways to counteract this.

Don't be tempted to say that you have considered the risks and decided that there are none. Sorry, that doesn't count and isn't true. It is almost a case of trying to find as many as you can, because this then demonstrates how carefully you have considered your setup.

Remember that having found a hazard you then need to fix it. Putting up a sign, providing appropriate equipment or training your staff are often the best solutions. It's a kitchen, which is an inherently dangerous place to work, so training is important here.

If you are an NCASS Member, this is included in your welcome pack. If not, I would recommend an internet search for "food business risk assessment template".

7. HACCPs

This is the food safety part – effectively your cooking risk assessment. The acronym stands for Hazard Analysis and Critical Control Point. It's a system for identifying the critical steps in food preparation: the moments when your food would actually cause harm if consumed. It's about staying aware of the hazards and preventing them from causing problems, because incorrectly prepared food is just downright dangerous.

Not only that, every time a street food trader causes food poisoning it sets the whole industry back a step, as the public's trust is shaken. It's worth getting right, so go for being obsessive about cleaning, and we will all thank you for it. Again there are lots of templates you can download for this. The government issued "Safer Food, Better Business" is probably a good place to start.

If you are an NCASS Member, a template is included in your welcome pack.

8. Cleaning Rota & Temperature Records

This is included within Safer Food, Better Business and within your NCASS pack, but depending on the format you will need one for every day of trading or one for every week. It's a check list of cleaning jobs and temperature checks, which in the event of a food poisoning incident form part of your "Due Diligence Defence".

What this means is that you have done everything in your power to prevent accidents from happening, and you have the records to prove it.

I would recommend writing your own. It demonstrates that you have looked at your setup critically, and thought about the cleaning process. Write down each piece of equipment, your surfaces and (if applicable) the floor. Add any additional jobs that you need to remember, like topping up the hand towels, sterilising the water bottles or making sure you lock the fridge before driving away. This is a document to USE, not just to satisfy the Environmental Health, so include jobs you want to make sure get done each time you trade.

Format it onto a table on Excel or similar, twiddle it so everything fits on a page of A4 and can be ticked, dated and signed for each time you're out.

Photocopy or print off a bunch of these and add them to your paperwork, then make it part of your setup routine to fill in one of these once you are assembled and cleaned down, but before you start cooking. Fridge and cold box temperatures have to be checked at least twice a day, so get used to forming habits early to avoid missing checks. Fridges that have a built in temperature display are excellent.

9. Method Statement

This is a document you will only be asked for on rare occasions, but thankfully it's something you only have to do once. You are effectively tying together the gap between your risk assessment and HACCPS, so all the bits that are not covered by one of the above.

It involves things like your arrival on site, the setup and who is in charge of an initial risk assessment, how you will make sure your unit is clean, your food is being served at the correct temperature and how you dispose of waste. It is a messy document that you may well never look at again, but is there to satisfy the gods of health and safety paperwork. It's tedious, but you just need to get a mug of tea and power through it.

As yet there are very few templates available online. Without one, you can still create this document. You need to run through an average day of trading as if you were the world's most finickity health and safety inspector and were deliberately trying to find fault, just to make life harder. Now list how you do all the jobs in your unit. Here's what you need to include, but the more the merrier:

- Contact information. Especially a mobile phone number that will be available during the event, and your business name and unit type.
- Identify the separate areas of your business. I've listed them below, feel free to add more. In each case identify the hazards first, and then describe your process for that area, in such a way that it will prevent these hazards from being dangerous.
- **Arrival and setup**.
  Hazards: moving equipment, gas safety, and inclement weather.
  Process should include: Looking where you are going, warning others, only allowing those specifically permitted to set up the gas to do so and testing it, securing your unit carefully.
- **Cleaning**
  Hazards: hurting yourself (both with chemicals and on sharp surfaces), chemical contamination, slips and trips.
  Process: provide gloves, train staff to use chemicals safely and tidy away food before cleaning, mop up spills immediately and leave unit free of obstructions.
- **Food Preparation**
  Hazards: Knives, food contamination, allergen control, gas and electricity injuries.
  Process: Train staff to use knives, use colour-coded chopping boards, clean down after using potential allergens and only allow trained staff to use cooking equipment.
- **Food Service**.
  Hazards: Contaminating food with money, passing customers food that is hot and therefore risk burning them.
  Process: using separate hands or handlers for food and money,

warning customers if food is likely to be very hot, wrapping food in protective packaging.

- **Pack Down and Departure.** Hazards: Mostly as with arrival. Process: tidying up after you, disposing of rubbish in the designated area.

As you can see, it's a massive waste of time. But it does encourage you to think about the process of cooking and serving which, pain in the butt though it may be, might make you realise that you are inadvertently doing something dangerous.

Again, if you are an NCASS Member, a template is included in your welcome pack.

Having Your Business Inspected by the Environmental Health

This is the scary part. Be nice. Generally speaking, only chefs with dirty kitchens hate the environmental health. Squeaky-clean kitchens (with the correct documentation) have nothing to fear.

There will be at least two inspections of your business, one preliminary before you start to trade where the Environmental Health Officer will come and look round, have a chat and give you advice on the next step. The part to remember is that this visit will not result in a rating. It means that if there is something you don't know, get wrong or have missed, you won't be lumbered with a terrible rating right from the start. Instead they will help and advise you on work that needs to be done. It's all very civilized really.

To prepare for this visit it is still worth having your unit set up, spotless and ready, in the back garden or on the drive. Phone them up and ask if they would like to see it. If everything is acceptable then they will allow you to trade directly after this meeting with the status "awaiting rating".

In our case we did not know until this first inspection that we needed a gas safe certificate on all our gas appliances. A bit of a surprise, but it meant that we were very much not able to trade after that first inspection. You're already ahead of us there. Nice.

If you have everything ready, and all your equipment is good to go then they may give you the all-clear - pending a rating.

Good News

This is good because you can get straight out there and start selling.

Bad News

Everyone will keep asking you what hygiene rating you have.

Environmental Health officers are not just going out inspecting restaurants. They have a lot of other jobs besides, and since the recession hit and many were laid off, this workload has increased. There are not as many inspections as there once were, meaning that if you can manage to impress the EHO with excellent records, a spotless kitchen or unit and thorough procedures they will probably leave you alone for a good while.

Your Unit

Unless all your cooking takes place inside your unit when you visit an event, it will be your prep kitchen that is most likely to be scrutinised. If you are planning on running the business from home, which you probably are, at least in the short term, then this means your kitchen.

Do make sure that you kitchen is spotless when the EHO come round, but don't worry about having it 100% up to standard. Talk to your EHO on their first visit and use them to work out what needs to be done. They are, contrary to popular belief, there to help you trade safely, rather than to stop you from trading at all. Don't aim to fly through that first inspection, aim to ask them all the niggling questions specific to your setup that a book, no matter how detailed and thoughtfully written, could not hope to answer.

Your Paperwork

The Environmental Health Officer will want to see your food hygiene certificates, your risk assessment, your Gas Safety (if applicable), your cleaning rota and your HACCPs. If you have specific questions about writing them don't be shy about asking, but you need to have had a good stab at producing these documents before your first inspection.

April 2011

The sun had begun to shine by the time we were taking our first steps towards being a proper business. We had submitted our licence application to Warwick District Council and we hoping for acceptance, but not entirely sure what that meant. I was panicking about getting everything right; terrified that one wrong turn could mean the end of the unsightly yellow creature on our drive.

Luckily our offer on a new house where we could store the business had been accepted, and we were planning to move. I would not recommend planning a house move in the middle of the opening phases of starting a business, but we hadn't either. It had become a necessity since the landlord randomly decided he didn't like a business for insurance reasons.

First though, we needed to make sure that the Beast would make a good impression in his new home. He was rather bright, and we had decided that our van should be green. After a little research we specified deep Brumswick green, being both nicely dragon-like and also gently Victorian-industrial. Had we still been planning to serve Victorian Street food, which we were not, then it would have been a smashing colour-scheme. Instead it became our colour. Recognisably Jabberwocky, rustic and easy to match with garden furniture and fence treatments, should the need ever arise.

We invited a bunch of friends over, handed them sand paper and beer, and let them get to work. More friends arrived, more beer was consumed, and the van was sanded down before lunchtime.

Impressed with the progress and lucky enough to have randomly picked the only sunny day that year we pressed on, and started getting busy with the paint. We were using coach paint, originally designed for horse-drawn carriages and by appointment to the Queen for fixing up the royal run-arounds. It's pretty good for metal, and gives a lovely glossy finish if you get it right. We were bribing friends with beer, so we didn't get exactly the glossiness we wanted, but we did get a bunch of extra character.

It meant that when we moved house a few weeks later and arrived on our new driveway, the Beast had already taken his final form, and would no longer be a giant graffiti-clad canary. Instead we needed to make him ours, and that meant getting some design work done.

Branding and Logos

While I don't think you have to have a logo to be able to trade, you will find that a lot of places seem to need one these days. Twitter and Facebook are prime examples of this. I'll deal with them specifically later, but you should know that advertising in street food is done on the web. It's not really a surprise, everything is done online these days, but you need some sort of online presence, and for that you will need two things you won't have: a logo and photos of you trading.

The catch 22 of this industry is that you can't trade until you have photos, and you can't have photos until you trade.

Here's what I'd recommend. You already have a rough idea of what your unit will look like, you have a plan for what you will serve and you have a name for the place. I imagine you also have a figure in mind to spend on branding and logos. I expect it's probably somewhere around £0. Unfortunately design is very much one of these "you get what you pay for" industries and with no investment you are unlikely to score a beautiful design.

Instead, tap into your friends and contacts. See if you have anyone who could design a logo for you. If you have any sort of design skills then do it yourself. All you need really is a placeholder, so that twitter isn't just an egg in some clouds. It makes sense to get the branding right if you are going straight for street food world domination, but in that case you really should have a slightly bigger budget. Our logo was designed by a friend who happened to also be a graphic designer – we are eternally thankful that we have such excellent friends – it was exactly what we wanted.

You can get away with less though. The reason is that you are not going up against global brands and massive advertising budgets. The competition consists entirely of people like you. Admittedly there are rumours of the big chains looking hungrily at the street food bandwagon, but at the moment we are blissfully unique. In practical terms this means that spending thousands on advertising won't really get you that much further ahead. It's the difference between winning a gold medal by 10 minutes or .003 seconds: It's still a gold.

Once you have one, this logo needs to then go straight onto any online homes you have been building, and then you need to find a way to get it on your stall. People will search the web for you once they have enjoyed your food, so they need to be sure that they have found the right people.

The simplest solution is to get that logo and your name on your unit. If it's a gazebo, get a vinyl banner to go across the front. They cost next to nothing on Ebay if you provide the design work, and many companies will even do basic designs in the price. With vans and trailers you can get vinyl stickers applied to the outside.

May 2011

We had already owned the van for 5 months. In that time we had moved house, painted him a different colour and I had made some excellent contributions in the field of street food blogging. But we were no closer to getting that first event. It began to become apparent that festival organisers do not find you, you find them.

I wasn't sure how to fix this, as we had sent out applications in every possible direction and didn't seem to be getting anything back. We were at a bit of a loss, so I decided to improve the website so that we could score business from the internet instead. At that time we were planning on running the Jabberwocky as a three pronged business: Selling street food at markets across Warwickshire, catering private functions with a British inspired, non-street food menu and selling Barny's cheffing services in people's homes, where he could cater for them directly.

Two of these services would have to be marketed on the internet, so having just about mastered the basics of web design; I set about teaching myself search engine optimisation (SEO) as well. This is the black art that decides which websites are spat out after you put a search term into google. It's a complex and ever-changing discipline, so anything I tell you here will be obsolete by the time you read it, even if you're actually standing here reading over my shoulder. Instead let me tell you about the internet at large.

Websites and Online

Most street food traders do not have more than a single page website. To be perfectly honest, this is all you will ever really need. When the computers eventually rise up and take over they need to know where to find you, and in that respect you will already be covered.

Our website is very much the exception to the street food rule. It's got a few hundred pages of blog sitting behind it, talking about everything from lighting to why I wanted a gold bin in my bathroom, and consequently causes us to rank fairly well on Google for all manner of random terms. But this is not what you should be trying to do.

You need two types of traffic to be able to find you on the web. This first is those people who have seen you trading live. They will almost certainly google [yourname] [yourfood] and see what they can find; Jabberwocky toasties, for example. The other, more elusive type of visitor, are those looking for a street food caterer for their event. People who want to find *somebody*. They will search for street food, mobile catering, wedding food vans and all manner of other terms, most of which are highly competitive and location specific. If you want to chase private events in this way then you will probably need to hire a decent SEO company and invest in a good website.

To be perfectly honest, it's not really worth your effort in the first year or so. While private events are an excellent way to add extra income without paying pitch fees, they will not be regular enough that you can get away without the regular markets, and they do require a lot more organisation. Your time is better spent getting some business cards made up, which you can then hand out to interested parties in person when the occasion arises. This is a much more solid way to get the private events, as you can sell yourself in person, and let your food do the talking.

When we started out in business I built a website for the Jabberwocky before the vehicle itself had even arrived. I was already blogging about the process of setting up a business and didn't even know what kind of business I was trying to set up. For us, having a website was part of the whole experience of running a business. On the other hand, I come from a family of computer programmers and consider myself to be reasonably computer literate. If you would like to have a website, then unless you know what you're doing, I would recommend the following.

Sign up for wordpress.com. It's free, and can be easily shuffled around with no prior knowledge, as long as you are happy to have a bit of a play. Pick the shortest web address that still includes your business name, location and/or food, select a theme you like the look of and you're basically already there.

Create a homepage with some pictures, your newly minted logo and your contact details. Be sure to mention [yourname] and [yourspeciality] in the title, the page description and the actual body of the text. No novels needed, just tell people what you sell, where you sell it and how they can get in touch with you. Then get someone else to read it through for spelling mistakes. Websites with spelling mistakes are a turnoff, and send customers elsewhere.

Don't feel compelled to go beyond that first page unless you have something totally new to say, because content can get thin very quickly out in the forgotten wastes of old websites. It's another turnoff that will scare potential customers away.

If the internet is a terrifying place then there are companies out there who will build you a tiny little one page site for around £150.

This will give you that all-important web presence, but it won't be much more effective than the wordpress one you could have made yourself. In this business you very much get what you pay for, and unless you have the resources for an all-singing all-dancing wonder-site a little bit on wordpress is all you will ever need. Plus you can edit it whenever you like to add new events or even take up blogging, and if you would like a custom URL (web address) then wordpress will do that for you as well for an additional fee. It's also one of the easiest platforms to get your head around, and you will be hard-pressed to actually break it.

Social Media

This is probably the best value-for-money advertising you will be able to get, so signing up for Facebook and Twitter is a solid time investment as long as you are happy to keep them both up to date.

Twitter

This is the preferred street food marketing mechanism. The type of people who use twitter are also the type of people who eat street food, and the conversational aspects of it, which allow dialogue between companies, their followers and other companies are superior to Facebook. It isn't universal though, whereas the entire universe and their respective dogs are on Facebook. If you can muster the energy to populate both with inspiring, unique and thought-provoking content about your food then you have probably won the internet and can live happily ever after, but in practise that's quite a lot of work.

Instead it might be worth setting twitter up to post updates to Facebook, so you can send content across automatically whenever you tweet. How this is done will vary depending on Twitter's current layout, but it's in settings – Apps at the moment.

The reverse is also possible, but the problem here is the character limit on twitter. You might post a quick update on Facebook which just goes over the character limit, meaning that twitter shortens it to a link. Your eager fans then have to click that link to see the end of your update, after first logging into Facebook, only to find it was just an extra word. Mild annoyance ensues.

Talk about what food you are cooking, tweet pictures of things you have seen and use a few hashtags to spread the love. Try to get into the habit of reading twitter and following local people and businesses, as well as the big voices in street food. Engage in conversation, respond and be generous (but not over-generous – no more than one retweet for every two pieces of your content) with retweets and your followers will grow naturally.

Facebook

Generating your initial audience here is easy. Set your page up and then ask friends and family to join. Facebook have even added a button to allow you to specifically pester people who might give you a follow. Growth beyond that is much harder though, because the conversation isn't as natural.

You know those buttons on people's website that link through to Facebook? You need one of those. Search "Embed Facebook "like" button" for a guide. Then and actually ask people to like your page in your online presence and on twitter. As long as people can find your profile they will seek you out and like your page if it has faintly interesting content, so there's no harm in getting it set up.

Food pictures are always good for Facebook. Anything visual might get you a share, and anything written might get you a like. Any interaction is good though, so talk to people and make sure you have it connected to a smart phone via the Facebook Pages app. This is the place where complaints will show up, if there is a problem. Dealing with them quickly and generously will save you a whole world of pain.

Other Platforms

There are lots of other platforms that you might want to put time into if you get the chance.

Instagram. If you don't take a good picture then this one is, without wishing to sound mean, a good place to start. The built-in filters mean that your slightly crumby shot is magically transformed into a moody work of #foodporn, and can then be shared on twitter or directly. Again this is a popular haunt for bloggers and foodies, and a strong following here will prompt more people to take pictures of you and your food. It's a great way of encouraging delicious free advertising. Instagram is currently still growing, unlike some of the other social leviathans out there, and as an added bonus: negativity very rarely crops up on Instagram.

Google+ If Facebook ever dies; this is probably what will replace it. Whether you can be bothered to populate it with content for the three users there at the moment is another matter, but it's probably worth keeping an eye on.

Pinterest is a great platform for sharing other people's stuff. If you have a blog and take a half decent picture then it is probably worth signing up and occasionally pinning, if not then it isn't worth your effort. That being said a lot of food bloggers use pinterest, so this is a good place to connect with them. They will appreciate a follow and may subsequently seek you out and try your food, but you will probably need some nice pictures to back this up. It is a good place to look for food-based inspiration. Every photogenic idea ever conceived is pinned here somewhere, so you need never think creatively again.

A blog. Worth its own category as a social media platform, and it's one that's very dear to me. Apart from being fun and therapeutic if you do like writing, a blog is a good way to establish yourself in the industry. You can share insights, give advice or just post cat pictures; it really is up to you.

As a means of promoting your website and business, blogging is also an important tool. When you generate content (write and post articles or stories) you are associating your site with that topic. Search engines notice and are more likely to send traffic your way. This is Search Engine Optimisation (SEO) in its most simple form.

All the benefits aside, regular blogging is a huge commitment that simply isn't worth the time investment unless you enjoy it. I update the Jabberwocky Soliloquy around once a week, and purposefully clear an entire evening for the job. While a weekly blog is far more than you need, you should really be looking at a monthly post or more. If you cannot commit to that then I would not recommend setting one up, as a dead blog makes it look like you're no longer in business and it can affect how well you show up in searches, because search engines also think you've stopped trading.

June 2011

June was the first time things finally started to come together for us. We had spent the first six months of the year trying to work out what we were doing, why we weren't getting work and how the whole business fitted together, but without any success in actually getting work. On the whole this was probably quite lucky. The van couldn't move under his own steam between January and March, and after that we still had a long way to go before the parts of him we wanted to cook on were actually legal.

Our first inspection by the EHO told us that we needed a gas safety test and to fix or remove all the dangly electrical wiring. We thought the wiring might be a problem, but the gas test was news to us. I'm very glad we found out then, because when we eventually found a gas engineer he thought the existing gas work funny enough to go fetch a mate so that they could laugh at it together. They then solemnly informed us that no, it was not going to pass. Nor was the dodgy grill, or the cooker we had hoped to replace it with.

The whole lot, both gas and electric, came out. In its place went a lot of new pipework, some nice sturdy wiring and a brand new cooker, which didn't quite fit the gap but did at least give us something to cook on. It meant that for the first time since buying the van we could theoretically take a booking which would require him to be present, functioning and safety tested.

We began looking for work in earnest, determined that the Beast should at least attempt to earn himself a living before the season was over. Most festivals like to get their catering sorted early on in the year, because it is the fees from your pitch that will pay for the entertainment. Markets don't book for the entire year, so if you are late to the street food party, that's the place to start.

Our first event was thankfully local, popular and well visited, which is the very best kind of event there is. It was the Leamington Food Festival, who offered us a pitch because we seemed like nice people, we were from just down the road and at the time we were serving something totally unique.

The Leamington Food Festival is free, held annually in the centre of town on the first weekend in September and attracts around 20,000 visitors with numbers growing steadily. It would later become a bit of a street food social, where all the best local vendors would come to sell food and share gossip. In 2011 it was to mostly just us, with our restaurant-inspired-miniaturised-dishes-to-go.

Working Out Your USP

Your Unique Selling Point is the thing that sets you apart from every other trader out there. It's the reason why an event organiser will choose you rather than the guys next to you. In terms of actually getting an event it is probably the most important factor out there, so before you start applying for events in earnest you need to have this one worked out.

The reason it's so important is that, unless you are a celebrity chef, the person booking the catering will not have heard of you. Sure, Jamie Oliver can show up and sell the stuff he found in the lint filter of his tumble dryer for £8 a pop, but that's really not something we can all get away with. Knowing what event organisers are looking for is important here.

- They don't want duplicates
- They want something visually appealing
- They want something that sounds tasty
- They want it in that order

The most important factor, as the person booking the food, is that you have *no more than one of everything*. At a bigger festival this becomes *one of everything in each area* and at a free food festival it usually becomes *not too many of everything*. If you book three hog roasts then the audience who fancies a hog roast will be split three ways. If you only book one then after the queue reaches a certain length people will almost unconsciously change their minds about how badly they want pig-in-a-bun and eat something else.

It is the best way to make sure that you can provide a varied food offering, and that the variation will still get a reasonable share of the

76

trade. As I've said, the hog roast will always do really well, but while punters will complain that there is not enough variety, they usually won't complain that queues were too long if there were other food outlets with shorter queues: they'll just get something else, and might even discover a new food they would not have otherwise sampled.

Knowing that, you see that when it comes to getting into that all-important first festival, you really need to be different. You won't be able to establish yourself as the regional hog roast magnate, and I'd argue that if you're reading this book that isn't what you had in mind anyway, so you need to be unique instead. These are your options:

The Food
There are several different approaches, but the most significant one is the food. Serve something that no-one else serves and you have an instant USP. If you have not already done it, now is probably a good time to search "street food[your area] [your chosen food]". If nothing relevant comes up try it a few different ways: [your wider area] and [a different way of describing your food]. We might start with "street food toasties Warwickshire" and then substitute toasted sandwiches, Midlands and mobile catering.

Go back a few pages and see what you can find. If there are dozens of different people offering the same service, or even one who dominates that area and seems to be everywhere, then it might be worth reconsidering your food. The brutal reason is that you will be surplus to requirements if you are trying to serve the same food at the same events, even if you are doing it better than they are.

It doesn't mean that you can't have competition though. In the Birmingham area there are lots of people doing great Mexican food. They all have a slightly different take, different setup and make a different burrito. As a result, while they won't get the same gig doing the same food, they all have a great following and all trade regularly. Another example is Meat Shack and the Original Patty Men: Two amazingly filthy burgers, but in the wider Birmingham area there is still plenty of work for both.

If you do still want to go ahead in a crowded market that is, of course, up to you, but please don't expect help and advice from the people whose turf you are hoping to mow. These guys are in business. If you set up a rival company serving almost the exact same food then that will reduce their business. It's unlikely they will welcome you into the fold.

Festival organisers will also "already have a tumble dryer-lint guy" and won't want to replace their established, reliable trader with you; a complete unknown. It can be done, but you are setting yourself up for a much harder and potentially more costly battle. To get into these events you will have to offer a better deal than their current vendor to win the pitch. This might mean tendering more (offering a higher pitch fee) or getting luck one year when they were let down by last year's tumble dryer lint guy.

If you choose to sell an untested cuisine (or untested I your area) setting up a business selling something interesting means that, assuming you have a reasonable street food community nearby, you will be the one everyone wants to try. This means traders and foodies alike will seek you out and try your food at least once which, due to the delicious nature of your food, will of course be all you need to get them hooked.

Without that street food community, far-out food will be a harder sell. I'd still say you can make it work, but the road will be a little longer than if you can join a city-based collective or event.

The Unit

There are alternatives to a unique food offering. While I would always recommend trying to serve something different, you can also serve the same thing in a different way. Having an eye-catching setup might be what you need to win over a festival organiser who had a so-so experience with last year's lint fluff guy.

Eye catching means that you either need to put a lot of thought into your gazebo setup, or you need to get a trailer or van. If you're getting a van, you need to be looking at the characterful end of the spectrum, where things get unreliable and expensive very quickly. The instant choice here is the H-Van – a sweet little French number produced by Citroën in the middle of the last century. They ooze character, but these days, in the author's personal opinion, they are decidedly samey. I would strongly encourage using your imagination and really hunting, rather than buying straight into the (thoroughly overpriced) H-van lifestyle.

A trailer is easier to decorate, so that might be your best option. If the festival organiser thinks they can get some potentially good sales shots of happy customers nearby, they will probably want to book you.

The Method

Lastly you have the same product, but done in a different way. This is probably going to be less visual to the organiser than the two previous methods, but it will set you apart from the crowd in the long term, if the end product is actually better. Our method for making toasties is unique to us, as far as we are aware. We think it also makes a better toastie, but we're really biased there.

You can also go for having a secret recipe for your chosen food, or you can make sure your sourcing is better than anyone else, or you can take a familiar concept and give it your own personal twist. Sure, we've all tried lint fluff, but have you ever tried it with poached pears and chilli sauce? The last option is the most saleable here, because with enough creativity you really can turn this generic food into something totally different, just be warned: flavours still have to sell. Mango and marmite might taste amazing, but you won't sell it without handing out a lot of samples. It sounds gross.

The Triple

Ideally you want to be targeting all three. If you have memorable food, a photogenic unit and you're making it in an exciting, new way then you should do better than those who are not. You will get into festivals more easily and should find that trade verses a comparable foodstuff is also better.

You biggest challenge will be finding a way to describe that food to organisers in less than 100 words. Our second concept, gourmet toasties, is easy enough. Our original idea "restaurant food that comes in miniature portions but is still tasty and delicious, like mini pie and mushy peas or cream cheese stuffed savoury profiteroles" really isn't.

On the other hand it did get us into quite a few festivals once we had managed to explain it. The reason we gave up on it was that it took us a week to prepare all the food for a single day of trading (To grade it in the same way as other food types: Prep time – Ultra high, service time – low, ingredients – medium with high wastage). Not even a very good day. It had to go.

Getting Started – Summary

Important achievements to have mastered by this stage should include having setup and registered a company, having decided what you are going to sell, how you are going to sell it and what your first events could be. Having those things as fixed points will help you work out the remaining details, because you know what you're working towards.

Chapter 3

Building up to your First Day of Trade

July 2011

This was when we had an email through confirming our very first festival. We were to trade at the Leamington Spa Food And Drink Festival on the 10th and 11th of September that year. We were elated, but suddenly a whole new flock of jobs appeared, none of which we had really anticipated. We found that getting to a festival was a far more complicated that getting accepted to trade at one.

As it happens Barny also proposed, which meant that everything we got done during the period - from having our first confirmed booking up until we actually started trading - is tinted with a distinct rose hue. Rather than take you through the process of how we came to trade, which in hindsight was with an unmanageable menu and much wasted effort, I will take you through the way we wish we had done it back then.

How to apply to events

The First Event

If you can possibly manage it, make your first event a single day of weekend trading in summer, not too far from your house, with some good friends nearby. You will forget vital bits of equipment, so have someone on the end of a phone who can drive them to you. The single day festival also means you won't be camping, which adds a whole extra van full of packing and setup as well as extra stress and increased difficulty in getting additional supplies. This is why you should also be close to home. Summer trading means it is more likely to be a busy day, which is thoroughly rewarding and will make it feel like all the hard work has paid off.

The perfect event for first timers is your local food festival, and they will probably also accept your application, because they are actively trying to promote local food. Once you have the application out to them, start casting your net further.

Subsequent Events

Imagine you have everything ready and you are good to start trading. Don't worry if that isn't the case, finding events that will take new start-ups are hard, and you will work much faster if you have a deadline. As long as you are looking for events at least a month away you can get anything done, it might just be a mad rush.

With this "everything ready" attitude you need to get a wall planner for the year. Cross off weekends that are already booked with personal activities like weddings, holidays and birthdays, and you will be left with potential trading opportunities.

There will be *something* on every single weekend between May and September if you are willing to travel far enough. By this I mean some sort of annual event, festival, or show. These are the best place to start if you are still working full time.

We live in the middle of the country and therefore have the luxury of being able to trade in a 50 mile radius, but if you are more remote you may need to go further to fill the diary. Take the dates of each weekend, stick them into google and follow with "festival" or "event" (for example: 22 23 April Festival). You will need to work through a few pages of results, but should be able to find a couple of events that fit your criteria.

Repeat this process for every weekend, taking note of contact details and preferred application method as you go. Once you have a mostly full calendar, get applying.

The Application

Whether it's online, by email or snail mail, the organisers will be looking for the same things and will ask the same questions. A vast majority of festivals have a form online which can be downloaded, printed and posted back. Expect this to drift into the internet over the coming years, but in the meantime get some stamps in. This is what you will need:

- Photos of your unit (set it up in the garden if you have to or use concept drawings)
- Public liability insurance, gas safe certificate, PAT test, Risk assessment, food hygiene rating (they may also ask for other items – see health and safety on chapter 3).
- Exactly what you will serve. This is where your USP will get you a spot. Folks doing burgers will struggle here.
- Website/facebook/twitter – as this is rarely used in promotional material it is more likely they will use it to establish how legitimate you are. This is why I had it in the last chapter and why it's worth building.

There will then be various other questions to establish your suitability which will vary between events, but if you are doing lots of application forms I'd just copy/paste from a master sheet or write a draft email that you can adapt to each one. If you are not terribly confident about your writing then get a friend to read through your master application form.

If there is the opportunity then I would highly recommend adding a short letter to your application form. Think of it like a job interview. Explain in that how you would be an asset to the festival and why you would be well suited to the event, along with any special requirements (we are longer than the average vehicle and usually mention that). Here are some great reasons why you are fantastic people to have on board:

- We are local to festival X
- We have been visiting Festival X for years as patrons, particularly love how well organised it is and would like to try trading there
- We noticed on previous visits or on the website that you don't have anyone serving potato sculptures. You would like to bring your delicious potato sculptures to the next X Festival.

Keep it nice and concise and the extra effort might well pay off.

The Offer

You have found an event that matches the criteria, which is great. They have made you an offer, which is even better. Before you get too giddy with anticipation, give it a very quick reality check to make sure you know what you're getting yourself into. Here are things you need to look out for:

- **Pitch fees that are in excess of £300 a day**. Not that you should decline these events, but the organisers need very good justification for charging this sort of money.
- **First time events.** Again, this does not mean it will be bad, but it does mean nobody will know how many people are going to turn up. Could be 10, could be 10,000. The organiser will confidently give you an estimate, but they DO NOT KNOW until the day, no matter what they insist. Don't be afraid to ask for details about their advertising campaign.
- **Organisers asking for pitch fees before accepting your application.** "Put a cheque for the full amount in with your application" As a general rule, you should try not to send pitch fees until you are sure you have the booking. This means you're not financially committed until the last possible moment. These guys might turn out to be morons, or something better might come along. As a general rule, once they have your money, you will never, ever get it back.
  Do still apply, but include a polite note saying that you will be more than happy to send payment as soon as your place is confirmed.

- **Offers asking for payment for multiple events.** There are dodgy organisers out there. If they have not worked with you before they will want to test you out before committing to long periods working with you (especially with traders just starting out). You will also want to test them out, because unless you are familiar with the market, you don't want to be committing to months of them.
  Any organiser who is happy to take your money for multiple events without ever having met you is either very trusting, inexperienced or on for a con.

If you are giving up the full time job then you will also need to look at midweek and evening trade as an additional source of income. Midweek means markets. This means finding a market (google "farmers market [mycounty]") working out who runs it and applying to them directly.

The midweek trade is much slower, and you may find that your area does not support the kind of market that welcomes street food, but it is worth having a look. The application process for markets is the same, but generally speaking after you have submitted paperwork once, they will not need to see it again that year.

The evening trade will probably be in the form of street food events. Our one is Digbeth Dining Club, based in Birmingham. The best way to find yours, if you haven't already tracked them down, is probably on twitter. This is a small community, and we all follow each other. Start by following @jabberwockyfood and have a look at who we follow, then who they follow and so forth. Follow anyone who looks interesting and you will have a network of street food events in no time.

The Pitch Location
The location of your pitch within the event is crucial. If you can specify where you would like to go, this is the kind of pitch you will want:

- **With the rest of the food.** It may sound better to be away from the offering, to snag customers who are "over here", but in reality, you can't provide choice by yourself. Customers roam in groups, and usually divide and conquer at mealtimes. This means if there is one person in your group who doesn't fancy candied offal the entire group will move along with them, to the rest of the food

- *On* **a corner rather than** *in* **a corner.** You know how supermarkets strategically place food they want to push on the end of the isle? That's a great spot. In the far corner on the other hand, is not.
- **In a browsing thoroughfare.** Meaning you are with other interesting offerings. People browse much more slowly than they walk. This gives them time to read your menu and look at your unit. If you are on the way to the toilets the footfall might actually be better, but single-minded determination to pee will override any desire to buy food.
- **Somewhere with a view.** If you can look out, others can look in. This is where whipping out your giant board or banner really can sell your goods across a field. This also allows you to indulge your passion for people watching. Festivals are great for that.

An ideal pitch, for example, is on the end of a row of produce stalls, facing out over the main arena, with the rest of the hot food dotted nearby. Don't be afraid to put your concerns to the organiser if you arrive and discover yourself in a pitiful pitch. Have a look round, see if you can find a better pitch that is currently vacant and suggest that instead. For the sake of getting you off their back they may well agree. If they won't or can't move you then make your case strongly, politely and perhaps even by banging a quick email to the organisers. This gives you something to fall back on if you do have a bad weekend as a result of the spot and/or the lack of customers.

Deciding on your kit

You need to know what has to be inside your unit for service to run smoothly. Once you have all these things together I would emphatically suggest a dry run in your garden so that you know, for example, how to put your gazebo up and where your tables and appliances go. If you have the time and energy, get friends round and cook for them from your unit.

There will be lots of folks around to help on the day, all of whom probably know how to put your gazebo up, but they have better things to do besides assembling your kit. Watching you fail to assemble your kit is probably one of them.

In terms of where to find these things, that will depend on your budget. We bought the Beast off eBay, along with masses of our current kit. Had we known about them, we would have visited a catering auction, which I would strongly recommend for if you have a solid list already. You should be able to download a catalogue in advance, and can then plan your bidding before the event. Just remember you have to somehow get all your purchases home with you.

Cleaning and Hygiene

I'll start with this, because without effective cleaning you won't be able to do anything else. It's tedious, but once you get into the habit you won't really notice it. Here are the bits you need:

- A hand wash sink which is either insulated or heated
- Blue paper towels or blue roll
- Antibacterial cleaning spray
- Washing up liquid
- Washing up bowl
- Hot water
- Drinking water
- Hand gel

First and foremost, you need a **hand wash sink**. Some councils allow you to use hand gels while on site, but remember that you will be travelling around, and the moment you get out of your county the rule might change. It's also currently being standardized, so expect it to become mandatory pretty soon anyway.

Either way, hand gels will only kill bacteria on your hands, which is lovely, but after setting up all your kit, hauling it to and from your vehicle and cleaning everything down your hands are going to be dirty. Consider it an investment, display it somewhere that customers (and visiting Environmental Health Officers) can see and use it regularly with antibacterial soap.

A portable hand wash sink will cost anywhere between £150 and £500, depending on how high tech you are. As long as it dispenses hot water and collects waste water separately you're good to go.

Hot water in that sink is something that EHOs also check. Being as the temperature at which heat kills bacteria is actually higher than you can comfortably bear this does seem a little strange, but it can still dissolve grease and oil, which do all contain bacteria, so I wouldn't advise a blazing row with the EHO if they do find your water is stone cold. Hot water is much more pleasant for hand washing anyway, so just roll with it. You either need an insulated unit, a powered unit (batteries or mains) or you need to top it up regularly with water you heat on site.

The **blue towels** are one of the fundamental certainties of street food. No matter what you do, where you do it or who you do it to, you will need blue paper towels, also referred to as blue roll, at some point in the process. This is what you use for your final surface clean down before cooking and to dry your hands with, it being hygienically clean. It's blue because food isn't, so if you accidentally cook a whole one into a stew you should be able to find it again.

Blue roll is the best solution for a gazebo, because you can hang it up to the frame on a bungee cord and use as needed. If you are in a van then paper towels work out slightly cheaper, but you really need a dispenser if you don't want to spread a packet over the floor every time you use them.

Antibacterial spray, also called antibac or blue spray. It's basically the same as the stuff you buy from the supermarket, only it's blue. You will get through a few bottles a week in busy periods, so it is much more cost-effective to go to the cash and carry, get the concentrate and make up your own. Wholesalers all have own brand cleaning products that you can make up as needed, just make sure you buy the special bottles for it, because they tell you that it conforms to the European standards on killing germs and fungal spores (BS En 1276: 1997 and BS EN 13697: 2002). It's one of the things the EHO might check.

Washing up liquid. Nothing beats a bit of hot soapy water when it comes to getting the grot up. Combined with a washing up bowl and hot water you can blast every surface once you're set up, antibac over and dry it off. BAM, hygiene. Plus the washing up bowl is then a good place to put washing up before you take it home, or to do a spot of ad hoc washing up while you're there.

This is what you need most of the **drinking water** for. You should have at least 20litres of potable water with you when you trade, for general cleaning, drinking and (if you are that way inclined) hot beverages. Normally this just means bringing a 20l container with you and filling it up on site, but if you can fit a full one in your kit it will save you a journey once you're on site. If you're taking an empty one make sure you know you will be able to fill it when you get there.

I know that adding **hand gel** to the list basically contradicts everything I just said about hand washing, but it doesn't take up much room, so throwing one in your kit is worth the effort for those times when you forget the hand wash sink, or it explodes, the battery is flat, you forget a pan to heat the water or you find yourself caught short in some other way. I would still recommend hand washing somehow and then anti bac gelling after you get back to your unit.

Hot or Cold Storage
You should know what you're planning to sell, so this is the point where you decide how to cook it. There are two major ways to prepare street food.

1. Cook offsite and then reheat when you get there.
2. Prepare from scratch onsite.

Some will argue that for it to be street food it should have been cooked on the street, but no matter what you serve you will end up making some of it in advance, so I disagree with this. It would also seriously limit the variety available, so ignore the debate and choose what works best for your offering.

If you are cooking something that requires long hours in the oven or stewing pot then the decision is made for you: you need to cook the day before and reheat. Don't be tempted to think you can get up at 4am and do it on the day, you don't have time for that and besides, most stews are better on day 2 anyway.

With things that are assembled fresh according to customer specifications: Pizza, burritos and (to a certain extent) toasties you will have to prepare them during service, although much of what you put in them will be prepared in advance.

The difference this makes is whether you will be hot-holding or cold-storing. Cold storage at its most basic requires a cold box and some ice packs. If you have a van or trailer, get a fridge. Hot-holding requires bain maries (water baths) or other hot-holding equipment. It is much easier to keep something cold than it is to keep it hot; cold storage requires no extra power once the cold box is set up. On the other hand food that is already hot is ready to serve straight away, and service will be much faster.

I would ultimately recommend making the decision based on waiting time and taste, rather than ease. Let us take, for example, the mighty burger. It takes approximately 4 minutes to cook a 5oz burger from raw to medium. You can then leave it sitting on the griddle for hours until you are ready to serve it, and service will only take 30 seconds. Unfortunately that poor little burger will be long dead by then and taste of leather. Cook the burgers to order (or add one for every member of your queue) and you will be serving more slowly, but the food goes out tasting infinitely better.

Cooking Method

This is the main way you prepare your main dish, assuming that the food is not prepped in advance and then kept hot, as described above. In most cases the type of food you want to serve will dictate the cooking method: if you want to serve wood-fired pizza, you will need a wood-fired pizza oven. If you want to serve burgers, you're going to need a flat griddle.

If it's feasible, I would recommend getting an LPG gas appliance for your primary cooking. Electricity, you will soon realise, is surprisingly expensive. Festivals will charge you based on how many 16amp hook-ups you need, so if all your cooking is gas you only need one for lights and refrigeration. Any cooking equipment (griddles, fryers and other large appliances) will almost certainly need at least a 16amp feed per item. If you can manage it, try and run on a totally electric-free kit to save yourself time and money, and only bother with power if you're trading at night.

On the other hand, electricity can be used anywhere, including indoors. It does happen and will become more frequent as street food begins to pop up all year round. If you are considering a second setup, an electric only one might be a sensible choice.

Smoky cooking methods like BBQing are a brilliantly visual, but make sure you buy smoke-free or low smoke fuel. If you are gassing your neighbours they will have to complain, and ultimately you may well get removed from a show before you've even started selling.

Gas is not a wonder solution by any means. It's much more prone to blowing up, and due to ventilation requirement it is more exposed to the weather, which means temperatures fluctuate in the wind. On the plus side it is a lot more efficient at getting things hot that electricity. Make sure you check that you are buying LPG equipment rather than natural gas appliances, and have them checked annually by a gas safe registered engineer. That last part is also a legal requirement if the appliances are more than a year old, or if you have gas work (pipes) installed inside your van or trailer.

There is also a healthy dose of common sense required when using gas. You can get away with all sorts of things because the law here is not terribly well known, but please go for safe over easy: if one of us has a spectacular explosion it will make it much harder for everyone else. Here are my recommendations:

- If you are in a van or trailer, your gas work must be done by a certified Gas Safe technician.
- If you're in a gazebo, use one bottle for each appliance. Most festivals will still need to see a gas safe certificate, effectively for the appliance, so take it to a Gas Safe certified technician and get them to test it. Even if they won't do you a certificate, headed letter paper with their Gas Safe registration details and the appliance details should be enough.
- Keep the hoses short, and don't put them across walkways (I've seen it happen). Seriously, that is the mother of all trip hazards right there.
- If you're not sure, go to a gas safe engineer and get them to show you (connecting and disconnecting appliances, use of regulators, leak detection). Chances are you will find one while

you're hunting for cheap gas (don't buy it from a petrol station – it's stupidly overpriced) so ask them.

- Keep the bottles away from the customers, in a well-ventilated area.
- Buy a decent spanner for connecting and disconnecting your bottles. If you're trading with us you can always use ours, but this will make life a lot easier.
- Treat it with the reverence it deserves as a highly toxic explosive. It will cost you an extra few seconds just to think it through, but it might stop you dying.

Prep

You will need somewhere to prepare food. On average, most traders probably have around 2m of spare table length for assembling, amending and generally tinkering with food during service. This is on top of all the space you need for storing food (legally, it can't live on the floor) setting up your cooking equipment and having hand wash facilities. Cold boxes can be stored on the floor at a push, but ideally you want everything containing food to be off the ground.

Two 2 meter tables should set you up well enough in a gazebo until you figure out exactly what needs to go where. If you're going into a market then you get 3 meters of frontage and that's it, so you have to get everything into that space or less. Enjoy – this is why we have a van.

Electricity

Obviously there are some trades that can't get by without electricity. Coffee carts are available in the hand-cranked or gas variety, but they are expensive and rare. Similarly if you're doing anything with ice cream, smoothies or frozen yoghurt you will want to have power. If buying an ice cream van isn't an option, you are left reliant on the organisers or a generator for power.

At large events, all the power is produced by on-site generators, which have to be maintained all weekend by electricians. These guys are usually identified by a roll of blue cable over their shoulder and a slightly pained expression. They also universally wear cargo shorts and polo shirts. Even in winter. Pro tip: It never hurts to offer electricians a bit of free food. They do a fairly thankless job, are usually needed in four places at once and quite often don't get any food paid for while on site. Just supposing the power goes out it will be back online much faster if you have already had a chat with the guy you need to fix it.

When you apply for festivals the organiser will want to know how much power you need. A fridge, some lights and some fairy lights is about the minimum you can get away with there (doing the whole thing in cold boxes will require you to own a house full of cold boxes and freezer packs) and that all runs comfortably off the minimum amount available (1 x 13amp – the equivalent of a single plug socket at home). If you are running any other appliances this will usually push you over the minimum, and mean you have to start shelling out big bucks for power.

At any given festival you will usually find that someone, somewhere along the application line was a little creative about the appliances they planned to use. The first day will be spent with the electricity tripping for everyone while one idiot power-washes their fryer beside a junction box (actually happened – fryer was switched on). Please don't be that guy, the electrician will work out it's you, and you will end up only being able to use half your kit and the rest of us will not be impressed.

The other solution is that you have your own generator. Although you won't usually be allowed to use them at festivals (check beforehand) it is very useful to be able to power your entire setup, especially if you are looking to target the private hire, farmers markets or solo trading events.

Generators vary in price enormously, and you get what you pay for. Due to happy circumstance and lack of money we ended up needing only a 1kw genny, the smallest size you can buy, which will run all our lights and the fridge for most of a day. It's small enough that it fits in the van and can travel everywhere with us without getting in the way, meaning that in an emergency (arrive at a summer festival with a fridge full of food – no power for 6 hours) we can still keep ourselves going.

We use a silent petrol generator. They are widely available, the Honda one we use is ridiculously reliable, it's tiny and it really is pretty quiet. There are certain places where we can't use it, but on the whole it has saved us more times than it has been outlawed.

A non-silent generator will cost about half as much, and you can pick them up off Ebay by the crateful. The solve the problem, but the big generators are loud. Proper shouted conversation loud. If you can possibly afford it, it really is worth investing in a decent silent generator that you can just throw into your gear and forget about.

While we are on the subject of size, anything above a 3Kw generator will need more than 2 people to lift. Anything over 5 will be really hard to get in and out of vans. If you will be running the business by yourself then you are probably limited to a 3kw generator just for the sake of practicality.

When we first looked at the cost of power, and tried to imagine how they justified that extortionate cost, we initially wanted to provide our own. I would not recommend it. If you can take power from the organiser, it will always work out easier. It just isn't worth the extra hassle.

Top Tip: Get a 20m minimum 13amp extension lead and an adapter from 16amp (safe, waterproof blue cables) to whatever you're using. At festivals you will also need 20m of 16amp cable to get from their junction box to you (you can get it from Screwfix). No matter where you trade, people expect you to bring your own extension lead. Plus occasionally you can get free power from events when they suddenly realise they could just open a window and let you run an extension through. 13amp plugs are NOT waterproof unless clearly specified, so don't let them get wet.

Packaging

When we first started selling street food we had an eclectic menu of random restaurant food that was miniaturised and rearranged to be suitable for eating outdoors. This meant that on top of serving very prep-heavy food at a price which did not reflect the work that went into it at all, we also had to pay out for a whole variety of odd shaped boxes to serve it from.

People do not take time to marvel at your boxes. They eat t
food and the box goes in the bin if you're lucky. That's 12p you
never going to see again. It sounds silly, but in the grand schei
things, 12p is a lot. Just suppose you serve 2000 units this season.
That's £240 just on packaging. If you only paid 6p per box then you
are saving £120 just like that. Imagine all the shiny things you could
buy with £120.

So, when considering packaging for, for example, your Amazing
Cow Puffs, consider:

1. **Could you serve that tasty feast in a napkin?**
   This is as minimal as you can go: Better for the environment,
   cheaper for you, but harder for your customers to eat.
2. **Do you need cutlery?**
   I'm a staunch advocate of recyclable and compostable, so if the
   answer is yes, I'd recommend having a look on the web for
   non-plastic stuff. It is more expensive, but it's gone in a matter
   of months rather than choking the planet for millennia to come.
   If you don't need cutlery, don't provide it. People are prone to
   taking some just in case, and really don't understand when you
   try and tell them that actually this stuff costs you money.

You may also have no idea how to serve that food in a way that
customers can eat. If this is the case, try eating it yourself, while
holding a drink. Street food is often undertaken standing, so the ideal
scenario is that customers can eat your food without having to put
down their drink. Briefly passing it to a friend is fine, but the ultimate
food can be undertaken totally one handed, and packaging is key to
allowing this.

If one-handed is not possible, don't panic. Can it be eaten standing
up? This means the plate/dish/bowl needs to be solid enough that you
don't need a table to rest on and the food needs to be edible one
handed, without needing to cut it up, although dicing it with a fork is
acceptable.

I would try to avoid food that requires separate containers for
serving, unless they are all contained within a plate. Both from a
convenience point of view for the customer, so they're not juggling,

and to keep your costs down. If 10p of sauce always goes on the side in a 7p pot then that's just a waste of money.

Sourcing

The UK interpretation of street food has good quality built in. We need people to associate the term street food with superior quality for the industry to grow, so you will be doing us all a favour if you use decent produce.

Independent Suppliers vs. Wholesale

I would recommend that you source your ingredients from individual suppliers rather than using a wholesaler. Wholesale produce is not necessarily bad, and you will need to find and join the local cash and carry for a fair but of stuff, but it usually won't match the quality of the locally produced stuff and it has rubbish food miles, which do nothing for your green credentials. If you do go local, feel free to make a big deal of this though. Supporting your local economy is rightfully something to be proud of, so tell people on your menu that this food is locally produced and try and get some more information out of the producer. If you use rare breed pork make sure you know what the breed is. Otherwise you look silly when someone asks, which they undoubtedly will.

When we first started doing toasties we used Brakes for the bread. They're a national catering supplier and the bread is delivered frozen and utterly standardised. The bread itself was fine, there was nothing wrong with it, but it really wasn't special. The process of finding a baker involved going on google, finding local bakeries and then driving out there and talking to them in person. We eventually found a baker willing to work with us by spotting their van locally, and they agreed to produce the kind of bread we need. It works out slightly cheaper than Brakes. You won't necessarily pay more for local; quite often local producers are keen to get trade customers on board or the price from the big chains is what they know they can charge.

With us the bread was the most important part, and the first thing we started sourcing properly. We then went hunting for more suppliers and better produce, and these days I genuinely think we serve much better food because of it. I would recommend getting your main product right first and working outwards from there. Building a network of decent suppliers takes time, and often the only way to find out if they can cope with your needs is to use them. Discovering two or three bits of the supply chain break when you put in a large order could be really messy right before a big weekend.

Finding Suppliers

Actually finding your suppliers is quite hard, which is why I wouldn't try and get them all in place before the first day. Very few of them are online, most will only deliver within a certain radius and they might be unreliable because when you're a tiny company things can easily go pear-shaped. You will get to know that feeling.

Farmers markets are a good place to hunt because you can sometimes talk to the owner in person, so head down there armed with a camera and a clipboard, have some conversations and do a spot of shopping for quality control.

Asking another trader for their suppliers is frowned upon, I think mainly because it's about as technical as street food corporate espionage gets: We're all slightly paranoid that you will copy our product, and using the same produce is most of that. Either way, we put in the work to find them, so you should do the same. For that reason I'd expect an answer that is frighteningly vague, and would suggest you drop the subject. Instead keep your eyes and ears open and try google instead: [Your county] [produce to be sourced] usually gives you a few suppliers to start with, and there are also directories of farm shops and producers that might help as well.

Costing and Pricing Your Menu

Even if you love the industry and didn't get into it for the money, you still probably need to make some. We didn't cost our menu until months after we started to sell toasties, and discovered that a couple of our products were not remotely cost effective. There is no set ratio of cost price : sale price; you will need to work that out based on how valuable your products are perceived by customers and how much money you need to make for this to be viable.

Costing

Scrupulously collect all the receipts and invoices from produce purchased and keep a tally of how many units those bits make. Then work out how much it costs to make that entire batch and divide that by units on the tally. This is your unit price. You may have to wait until you are actually trading and buying in bulk for proper pricing, but don't forget to come back to it. Not only is this tasty data, it can be a nice surprise or a dire warning that you need to save money.

If you have multiple variations rather than a single product it is also worth calculating the cost of individual ingredients, which is what we do for toasties.

In a ham and cheese toastie there are two slices of bread, one portion of meat, one portion of cheese and an application of butter to each side. Working out the cost of these individually is a pain, because one 4 Litre tub of our homemade spreadable butterbutter will not always make the same number of sandwiches, usually depending on who is making the toastie, but we know that on average it makes around 300 portions.

Repeat this process for every single ingredient you use, even the cheap ones that you didn't think really cost you anything – do you squeeze a dollop of mayo on that granola-battered devilled kidney skewer? Then you need to know how many dollops are in a tub, and how much a tub of mayo is costing you. Spreadsheet that costing. Spreadsheet it hard and you will know exactly how much every single jalapeño slice is setting you back.

Once you have this glorious data you then know how much extras and substitutions cost, and you also have a good starting point for working out what to charge.

How about an example

Let us say - for the sake of argument - that you have chosen to serve a burger, which I pick not because you should, but because it's nice and easy to demonstrate additional costs.

I'm going to assume a street food attitude to sourcing, so prices will usually end up being almost the same or higher than you would pay for an inferior supermarket product, despite buying in bulk or making from scratch.

Here comes another table. I love these parts. This is The Imaginary Burger Company, who have just started out. Boy do they love sticking extra stuff in their burgers. One with Everything On It is the size of a small car – be we don't judge; their sourcing is spot on.

Product	Price wholesale	Portions per kg/l	Price per unit
Beef	£7/kg	Just over 7	£0.95
Bun	45p/Each	-	£0.45
Mustard	£3.97/litre	50	£0.08
Salad leaves	£3.40/bag	20	£0.17
Cheese	£6/kg	25	£0.25
Bacon	£8/kg	25	£0.32
Coleslaw	£2.50/kg	20	£0.12
Ketchup	£2.50/kg	50	£0.05
Relish	£6/kg	20	£0.30
Onions	£1/kg	15	£0.07
Gherkins	£2.50/kg	13	£0.08
Total			**£2.84**

I'm not sure how that stacks up with your expectations, but I expect it's probably more than you were really expecting to pay. Obviously there are huge regional variations on meat, and everything is dependant very much on how much of each ingredient you use, but the Imaginary Burger Company have just realised that because they sell their burger for £5.50 they are making less than 50% on each one. Now take away pitch fees (~20%), running costs (~10%) and you have about a pound from each unit sold to pay your staff, yourself and fund the next event.

Just to put that into context, at an average street food event or market you might shift 100-200 units.

Cash Margin vs. Percentage

When deciding on your price you are probably best thinking in terms of a percentage. It's easy to get seduced by the idea of simple cash profit: Imaginary Burger Co gets £2.66 of cash-money for every single one sold, but the problem is that your food ingredients are not the only thing you're shelling out for here.

We trade at a whole variety of events, who all charge different pitch fees. I'll go into more detail on the individual types later, but all of them, except the rubbish ones, will charge pitch fees. Sometimes the rubbish ones do as well. Those days are hard.

At any rate, you can expect the fees, regardless of whether they are taken as a fixed upfront fee, a percentage, a ration of free meals or a combination of all the above, to be somewhere between 10% and 25%. You can spot a bad event as one that exceeds 25% - a great one is under 10%.

If your food costs are 50% and your pitch fees are 20% - that leaves a measly 30% to cover everything else, including your wages. There is also VAT to consider, which I will handle in depth later, but just think about subtracting a further 20%. It doesn't make for fun accounting.

We will shelve VAT for the time being and concentrate on a practical example.

We do a regular market in the centre of Birmingham with pitch fees of £37.5, paid up front. This means that in order for the pitch fees to get down to 20% we have to take £187.50. For us this means selling around 50 toasties. We run at roughly 30% cost over our entire range, so on a bad day this would still be £96 of profit after pitch fees and ingredients. Imaginary Burger Co would only have to shift 34 burgers to get there. The sad thing is that once you take away the ingredients and the pitch fees, at the end of a rainy day when they only managed to shift 34 burgers (it does happen, far more often than most of us like to admit) all they get to take home is a rather thankless £56. Divide that by two people over perhaps 10 hours of work. That's £2.80/hour. Yippity do.

So you need to decide how much you want to take home. Don't base it on the bad events; you shouldn't be doing them unless you have nothing better on, but keep it in mind.

Perceived Value

Perceived Value is what will actually sell your food. A potential customer looks at the entire setup: your menu, the length of your queue, your unit & you, the location it is in, the food that is cooking and food that others are already eating. They then make a (largely unconscious) decision based on all these factors. If they judge the value to be high then they will be happy to spend more, so find that sweet spot where the price you are asking for exactly matches the amount they would like to spend for what is on offer. You want as many customers as possibly to leave thinking that your food was good value for money, and that does not necessarily mean cheap.

It will mean a little bit of experimentation and possibly different price points for different places. You can have the fanciest menu and nicest setup in the world, but if you are trading in a litter-strewn layby on an A-Road in the back of beyond then the location will devalue your offering before anyone even looks at the menu.

The is true for knock-down prices at a food festival. People expect the food there to be of a higher quality. If you are selling a wonderfully sourced gourmet bells & whistles burger for £2.90 the customer will assume it's going to taste grotty. You might be just trying to shift a few extra units.

Experimentation on price should be done over the course of several different trading opportunities, not at one event. Pricing plays a massive part in the perceived value, so people will assume that a £6 burger takes better than a £3 one. Dropping your prices half way through an event will really mess with this perception.

True Story: We were trading at a festival alongside a pasta stall. I've made my thoughts clear on pasta in previous chapters, and this really was a great example of poorly executed pasta. Big vats of shop-bought sauce, dried fusilli that was cooked, left to go hard and then occasionally brought back to life with a thorough dousing of oil. For a plate of pasta with sauce, a garnish of salad and chips they were charging £7.

It was a fairly sizeable plate of food, but the value didn't stack up, and people were not buying so business was slow over there. As an exercise we could even work out the actual cost...

Heading to the cash and carry quickly then: Pasta - 15p for 125g, 48p for 160g sauce, 32p for 200g chips, 20p for 50g salad. That's being generous, and ingredients cost £1.15 –well under 20%.

The following day the price had dropped to £5. People were outraged. Clearly the price dropping meant that the quality had been poor all along, and that they had been ripped off on the first day. We had people darkly warning us against the pasta, and declaring that they wouldn't even try it. The Moral of the Story: Be careful when and where you lower your prices.

Change

When handing cash, we don't deal with anything smaller than a 50p. It means all the calculations can easily be done in your head and it reduces your float as you don't need half a ton of change. I would highly recommend it.

Presentation and Setup

In terms of your looks, technically, you don't need any sort of pretty presentation for your stall, gazebo or setup. You will still sell some food. If it's good food, you will probably sell more of it, so don't panic about making your unit look visually outstanding right from day one.

There are a few things you can do to make it look nicer without spending a small fortune, which should increase your sales. Think percentages again. If each one of these points increases your sales by just 1% then doing all of them will give you an extra 10% mor effectively for free, forever.

- Make your cooking visual: Paella pans at the front or side of your stall rather than the back, samples and greenery out and the finished product on display (only do this if it won't look congealed and grotty after half an hour).
- Nice clear menus, so that people don't have to guess the next step. If your ordering involves a process (pick a bread, pick a topping and pick a dressing for example) then write a step by step guide. A piece of MDF, painted with blackboard paint, is an instant blackboard.
- A big sign stating what you sell in one or two words, which can be read from a distance. By all means have specifics in a smaller size; you could devote one third of the board to the words "gourmet Italian style, vintage wood fired oven hand-seasoned" and then in big letters finish with "Pizza". Although "wood fired pizza" might be snappier.
- Lights. I might even need a little rant to emphasise this.

Lights

The thing we had to learn the hard way about lights is that they are not there for you to see by. This is, at best, a secondary function. They are there so that you can be seen. You need enough lighting so that you look open. If you are trading in a van or trailer then it's worth having the capability to run lights during the day as well, especially when the weather is bad, so invest in a few decent, sturdy lights and illuminate yourself.

At night this is even more important, because you lose all your other visual decorations or signage. Warm white light (the stuff in a light bulb) is much better than neon strip lighting. It makes your unit and food look more appealing; just make sure you have enough that you give off light and illuminate your menu, rather than just enough to see by.

If you want to really stand out then waterproof fairy lights or rope lights will make your unit look pretty at night, but obviously they are one extra thing to pack, put up and take down.

One other point to consider with coloured lights: They can make your food look a little eerie. We have green lights on the van by day, because they stand out and make us look open, but at night we switch them to white to match the inside light, because otherwise all the food comes out bathed in an odd green glow.

Anyway, back to my bullet points:

- Keep your stall clean. This goes without saying really, but it's a nice simple one that doesn't cost you anything.
- Promote yourself. It's not something I enjoy, but it does help. If someone has said something nice about you don't be afraid to write it on a board and display it. Tweets are really good for this because they come limited to 140 characters as standard.
- Win an award. There are plenty out there, and most of them you nominate yourself for. No one else is going to do this for you, so be shameless.

There are other methods for increasing sales that are more expensive and may also have an effect, but it is very hard to test, because no two markets are ever quite the same. Anecdotally though, these seem to work.

- Trade from an amazing setup. It also gets you lots of free promotion because people will Instagram the hell out of you.
- Flags, banners and flyers. Undoubtedly helpful, but can be costly. I think that vinyl banners are nowhere near as nice as blackboards, but they don't run in the rain either.
- Uniforms. They look tidier inside the unit and more professional. You can do this cheaply by just buying a load of t-shirts in your colour, or you can have them professionally embroidered. Remember that if you are wearing a full apron all the time there isn't much point in getting embroidered t-shirts.
- Becoming famous. We would love to experiment with this, or give you advice on how to find a way in, but keeping your ears open and reading - rather than just posting - to twitter seem to be good places to start.

Writing your Menu

There is a bit of an art to this, ask any restaurateur. Keep it simple, get to the point and don't get waffle in the way of your food. Until we got a giant overhead sign proclaiming that we sold toasties we would often be asked if everything on the menu was a toastie. Admittedly we have always had a few sweet ones in there, and we tend to field some fairly exotic combinations, but obviously there was some confusion, and where there is confusion, people grip their wallets feverishly and scurry elsewhere. If you can manage never to be asked if you sell chips, that is when you know your menu is clear.

Descriptions

Consider your product. In this case we are embarking on a new venture to sell German dumplings – Knoedel [Kno-del], because they have a funny name, with a variety of different sauces.

As it's an unfamiliar product we have a separate board explaining the humble Knoedel (not even sure why it's so funny) to the masses and then our main menu again has "German Dumplings" written on it somewhere just to be on the safe side.

There are four different types of knoedel, each one matched to a different sauce: Steak knoedel & mushroom sauce, onion knoedel & tomato sauce, salmon knoedel & cream sauce and pork knoedel & creamed leeks. That's some fine hearty food right there. Bavaria would be proud.

You can either let people choose which sauce they fancy with their knoedel, which means slower service while you ask follow up questions but gives more variety, or you can specify those options right there. I would recommend taking a leaf out of the restaurant menu. The customer who wishes to mix and match will tell you anyway, so give your customers a dish to order (Steak Knoedel with mushroom sauce) and then sell it in a description:

Steak Knoedel with Mushroom Sauce
-28 day aged [local to this location] beef in a potato Knoedel with a champagne and chestnut mushroom sauce.

Onion Knoedel with Tomato Sauce
-Shallot and red onion bread Knoedel in a rich herb and tomato sauce with Somerset cheddar and crushed garlic topping.

The description is what adds the value here, and describing your ingredients means people know exactly what they're getting and might be able to overcome the fundamental problems of not knowing exactly what a Knoedel is. I'm also using ingredients that sound good on a menu if I'm totally honest. The description sounds tasty, and seeing as you are using the expensive ingredients you might as well flaunt them.

You can go too far on these, so as a rule of thumb you want to limit yourself to one description per ingredient used. As an example: crushed garlic is fine. Crushed, hand-picked Normandy-farmed garlic is a little excessive, and makes you sound like you have a tiny moustache, a pretentious sneer and a thesaurus up your butt.

Pricing

The Manwich has taught us a lot about pricing. This massive triple-decker sandwich sells for £7.50, and this means it is usually one of the most expensive items at any event. But it still sells. Even better: it makes everything around it sell too.

We first started noticing this phenomenon when trialling a £5 toastie. Seafood, game and other interesting ingredients could finally make their way onto the menu, and simultaneously the £4 toasties started to sell better. A little investigation and some trial and error show that the magical concept of "good value" is influenced by other items on the menu, so having something more expensive was, I suppose, both raising the profile of our menu overall and giving people a middle ground so that they could justify treating themselves to a more interesting toastie.

So you might want to consider a double Knoedel portion or an Uber-Knoedel for less than twice the price, because some people will spend the extra for a larger portion and there's money to be made there. Plus it might also help items in the middle price range to sell better.

Layout

This will only ever be important if you have more than three options on your menu, and we can again only back this up with circumstantial evidence, but here is the beef: The top item on your menu will sell disproportionately well.

106

For our first year of trading, the ham and cheese toastie lived at the top of the menu. Lowest priced of all our toasties, we kept it there so that people could quickly see a nice simple toastie, and so that prices increased gradually to the Manwich. Ham and cheese has always been the most popular toastie on the menu, so it seemed sensible to order it first.

More recently though we have been experimenting with the menu order, moving ham and cheese further down the board, to the bottom half. Sales dropped off on the ham and cheese, and picked up on anything in the top spot. As a determined menu reader it had never occurred to me that folks wouldn't get through all the toasties on offer, but would just pick the top one. This does explain a lot though.

So you might want to think about only offering three different choices, or accepting that the things on the bottom half will never sell as well. It's certainly worth experimenting with the order of things, ideally so that you can get the item that you think tastes best (or the one that makes you the most profit) into the top selling spot.

How many portions should I take?

I'll deal with this in more detail later, but for your first event, you need to take enough portions to potentially make some money. For that, you are best off using the percentage method:

The Percentage Method

The simplest way to judge an event is by how much you have paid in pitch fees. In an ideal world we would like to only pay 10% pitch fees, so that is your top end, now work out how many portions you need to sell so that the pitch fees are only 10%.

A low example.

The market is charging you £30 to be there. So for that to work out at 10% you need to take £300. You have an average selling price of £5, so that means you need to take 60 portions.

A high example.

This works on a grander scale as well. A music festival is charging £1500 to be there. For that to be 10% you need to take a colossal

£15,000. That means you need to pack – deep breath – 3000 portions.

I feel a disclaimer is in order: this does not guarantee you will actually sell 3000 portions, nor are the event organisers obligated to make sure you do, but it will give you a basic idea for the amount of portions you need. It is also much easier to hit 10% at smaller events, so you may want to aim closer to 20% at festivals.

Working out your portions long term is something to build up to. I'll cover it again once you're past the first day.

Preparing for Your First Day of Trading

The first time you go out and trade you will want to have as much of the actual food prep done as possible. Later, when you slip gently into a routine, you will find yourself arriving at these events with barely so much as a chopped onion, but that's further down the line. For your first event you want to arrive, set up and be as ready to serve as you possibly can be straight away.

This arguably gives more time for you to panic, worry and convince yourself that no one is going to buy anything. On the other hand it also gives you more time to dash home, get someone to do a supermarket run or mend the piece of kit that has chosen this exact moment to break. Don't worry, we've all been there.

Pack tea and coffee bits if you do partake in piping hot survival beverages, because the day will run on caffeine.

Write a list of the jobs you need to do once you get on site. It will be specific to your set up, so have a plan in your head, or draw a diagram if it helps, and then work out in what order you want to get from van-full-of-kit to street-food-stall-of-dreams.

Then have a brew.

You've successfully got this far. That's about 90% of the boring work out the way; you are officially onto the fun part. Your first event will be hard, but it will be fun as well, so don't worry. Here are some last week and last minute check lists to give you a starting point for getting your gear together.

The Week Beforehand Check List

Here are the things you need to have ready and up to date *before* the very last minute. Doing this the night before will not work, so make time for this before you are in the car, on the way.

- All your health & safety docs. Get a document wallet and put copies of everything in there. Keep that with your kit.
    - Public Liability Insurance
    - Daily cleaning rotas
    - Risk Assessment
    - Gas Safe
    - PAT Test
    - Food Hygiene Rating certificate
    - Personal food hygiene certificates
    - HACCPs
- A shopping list for the food you are planning to cook.
- A prep list of every cooking job needed before you can serve.
- Details covering when you need to be at the event, who to talk to when you get there (or just find someone in high-vis with a clip-board) and where you need to go (if it's a festival there might well be a different gate for traders).
- Floats. We run two cash belts with a £60 float each so that we can both take money: £30 in fivers, £20 in £1s and £10 in 50ps. What you need will depend on what you charge, how many people at your stall are taking money and whether you like scrabbling around for change last minute.
  For this first event: Make sure you have change.
- A list of the equipment you need to have with you. Here are most of the things you will need in an average setup, so this should give you a starting point for your list. All the asterisked items are either direct or indirect legal requirements. By indirect I mean that you need them in order to fulfil a direct requirement, like keeping food at a fixed temperature or measuring that temperature for your records.
    - Gazebo/trailer/van

- Primary cooking device: griddle, cooker, bbq, waffle iron
- Hot holding equipment (bain marie)
- Urn or saucepan for heating water for hand sink, cleaning and emergency tea*
- Gas bottles
- Generator & fuel
- Extension Lead and 16amp-13amp adapter
- Lights
- Uniforms or/and aprons
- Tongs or pallet knife for serving
- Packaging to serve into
- Napkins
- Something dispense your napkins and packaging from
- Disposable cutlery (if required)
- Chopping board(s)
- Knives
- Temperature probe*
- Spoons (especially if you have any sauces that are not in squeezy bottles), but everyone needs spoons.
- Disposable gloves
- Cold box & cold packs or fridge*
- Insulated or powered hand wash sink (and battery if applicable)*
- Antibacterial soap*
- Paper towels*
- Antibacterial cleaning spray*
- Banners & A-board
- Floats
- Tables (the minimum you can get away with here is about 3m of table length)
- Menu
- First Aid Kit for commercial kitchens*
- 20 litres of potable (drinking) water*
- Fire extinguisher*
- Fire blanket*
- Camera (or a friend who will come and take pictures for you)
- Health & Safety Docs*
- Rubbish bin & bin bags

The Day Beforehand Check List

This is it, the big one that you have been building up to. Have a cup of tea, sit down and check that you've thought this through.

- All the food is ready to go. Prep it as far as you possibly can to reduce the amount of jobs and panic required on the day.
- Phones are charged
- Directions to the place are on hand
- Everything is packed so that tomorrow you just jump in the van/car and go.
- You have friends on hand who can help out if you forget something (which you will).
- You have comfy shoes. It's a lot of standing up.
- Appropriate clothes. If it's raining in the morning while you're setting up you will be wet for the entire day. No fun.
- If you drive a delightfully unreliable vehicle, start it and take it for a quick 20 minute drive now, fully laden. You know it will then start tomorrow and you will have a feel for how it moves full of stock. At the very least, start it and let it get warm.

Chapter 4

The First Day of Trading

10 September 2011 – Leamington Spa Food Festival

The festival didn't start until 10, and we didn't need to be there until 9. It is less than 2 miles from our house; so naturally, we were up at 6:30 and ready to go. Last minute checks of everything were performed, and we scrambled into the van and trundled down there.

It was still grey and early, but we found our spot and set ourselves up. It was a little out of the way, just next where a large brand were setting up a stall and beginning to hand out pots of free food, but we remained positive. By 10am we were ready to trade, and had heated up our first few portions in advance of the crowds.

Ten minutes of confident waiting turned into 30 minutes of nervous anticipation. More and more people filed into the gardens, came down the path far enough to glance at our menu, and then scuttled off again. We gave the preheated food to friends, who had turned out in force to support our efforts, and insisted on paying.

30 minutes ticked into an hour, and we still hadn't sold anything. Each portion had taken so long to prepare we couldn't bear to throw them away, but we needed to be ready for that first sale, so we cooked more. I am prone to worry at

the best of times, but this was off the scale for me. Everything must be wrong.

Eventually then, when we finally made our first sale well after 11am, it was a huge surge of relief. The unsuspecting customer bought the carrot bhajis, and had no notion of the significance of his purchase until we told him. At that point I think he was kind of hoping we would give it to him for free. We did not, figuring to take that path would be a short, swift slide towards bankruptcy.

As lunchtime dawned across the park more and more people began forming queues at the hot food sellers, and we started getting intermittent sales. It was exciting, and to try and boost trade I got out there with some samples and started giving it away.

We rinsed through three or four portions of brownie and made a couple of sales off the back of it. People carried on buying our food, we handed out a few business cards and by the end of the second day we had actually sold out of carrot bhajis.

For a first event on a menu as random as ours it was a pretty good achievement. We covered the cost of pitch fees and the cost of ingredients, but we did not make enough to pay ourselves for the day's work. Or the two weeks of work that had gone into preparing for the food festival.

If we had known then what we know now, things would have been a whole lot easier. I'll explain.

What To Do On Arrival

Pulling up at your first ever event is daunting. Everyone seems to know what they're doing, there are people everywhere and most of them are ignoring you. Not to worry. This method should work every time:

- If there is security, they will have radios and be able to point you in the right direction. This will be the site manager or catering manager. You should have their name from the booking.
- If there isn't, find a marshal. Look for the nearest person with a high vis jacket and a clip board. They're asking for trouble.
- Tell them the name of your company and ask them to find your pitch. Buck conveniently passed.
- Head down there and set up in line with the caterers on either side. Don't be the ones who stick out.
- If you do find someone in charge, you need to get the following information out of them:
  - Stand pipe (fresh water) location
  - Power provision (when will it be switched on and how do you hook up)
  - Waste Water location
  - Arena opening & closing times (if you are not in a camping area) or trading times at a smaller event
  - Toilets
- Once you're in and have those details, you are set for the weekend. When exactly you trade after that is usually mostly up to you, as they will (probably) have a license for the entire weekend. It is usually not worth opening on the day before the festival, even though there are crew members on site. If you want to, it's unlikely anyone is going to stop you.

What we did Wrong

It's easy to look back on now; hard to see at the time. For the audience at home, here's what we got wrong.

We didn't have a clear product. Our menu consisted of the following items:

- Miniature pie triple and peas with gravy
- Carrot bhajis with mint raita
- Savoury pancetta profiteroles stuffed with cream cheese on a bed of rocket
- Chicken Caesar Salad
- Triple choc brownies with warm chocolate sauce
- Crème Brulee stuffed mini donut balls

So the food was pretty interesting, but the only description we could come up with was "miniature restaurant food to go" or "restaurant food street food style", neither of which immediately bring any sort of image of food to mind.

Fix it: Ultimately we changed product entirely and started to sell toasties, but on later outings we improved our description to "British Bistro Street Food" and ditched the idea of tiny. Don't tell customers your food is small, that's just not smart.

You couldn't tell what we were selling. At a distance of more than three meters it was difficult to tell if we were a food van, produce van or just lost, so from across the field you had no hope.

Fix it: Barny's dad made us a giant blackboard and we wrote "toasties" on it in big letters, once we started selling toasties. It's great to be coy, but do that once you're famous and don't want to take an unfair proportion of the crowds because of it. Then think WWJOD (What Would Jamie Oliver Do?) and get that massive great big board or banner.

Our food was not good value. Three minced-pie-sized savoury pies and a side of mushy peas for £3.50. All well and good, but the pies were gone in two bites and did not look like a substantial serving. Everything on the menu was £3.50, and then you could get 3 for £10, saving 50p. Throughout the weekend only 4 people took us up on this, most just eyed the food distrustfully.

Fix it: It really wasn't bad value for money, but if your customers think it is, you will still fail. Not having varied price points is a huge part of that, so we now offer everything from £2.50 right up to £7.50. Nuzzle up to their wallets and give them a price they want to pay.

The menu was far too much work. Two weeks. We both took an entire week off work and spent most of that time in the kitchen. The ingredients may not have cost us much, but we spent *hours* prepping all those fiddly little portions, only to have people tell us they were small. On top of that, because we had so much to prepare, a lot of it had to be frozen in advance so that it would still be fresh on the day. It then can't be frozen if it doesn't get eaten and had to go in the bin.

Fix it: Again, finding a food that worked for us was crucial. We didn't have a huge catering kitchen at our disposal, so the street food miniatures were never viable. Toasties need a lot less space. Also: don't be afraid to charge for the time spent making them. As a general rule of thumb, the cheaper the ingredients, the more work they need: flour is cheaper than bread. The pies only cost us 50p per portion, but that portion took 20 minutes to make. Which means after pitch fees (20%) and running costs (10%), I was paying myself £2 for 20 minutes work, not including all the time spent standing there on the day not selling them.

A toastie takes about a minute to make, but the ingredients are more expensive. It needs to add up to be viable.

We hadn't sold anything by 11am and panicked. And so will you. And we still do. The longer you have to stand there and watch the world go by, the more certain you will become that everything is wrong. Unless you find a distraction this doesn't ever get any better.

Fix it: If you're not selling specific breakfast food – and I mean bacon rolls or cooked breakfasts, none of this airy-fairy granola hippy-chow - you won't sell much before 11:30, and that's ok. Certain food stuffs will sell more before lunch than others, but anything considered "world food" won't really get a look in. So set yourself up, and then go for a wander, find some breakfast, have a brew, get to know the people nearby, put some pictures up on social media. No need to panic. Or sell breakfasts.

Where we Wasted Time and Money

Your first day of trading is the one against which all others are measured, at least to begin with. This will be when you are least organised and most likely to be floundering at the deep end. Everything should improve from there onwards, the weather excepting, so you can save yourself a whole lot of time and effort by not worrying about certain things in the run up to that first day.

You don't need an A-Board. No matter how often I mention it, it is not a standard by which other traders or events will measure you. We had one inside the van when we bought it, and spent hours painting it up and deciding what to have written on it the night before our first event. That sort of thing will come to you naturally out of conversations with customers, especially ones who tweet nice things about you on social media.

Uniforms were another place where we could have saved a load of money. Because we were heading down the catering route, and saw ourselves doing weddings galore in a year's time, we went for blouses and chef whites and then t-shirts for setting up and packing away. The t-shirts are all we wear now, partly because Barny is firmly of the opinion that ironing is a sinful waste of time, partly because blouses are just not street food.

Do plan to get uniforms at some point, I have no doubt that it emphasizes your brand and makes you look more organised (and therefore safer, the thought goes) but it will not make enough of a difference to worry about on your first day. Do make sure you have aprons though: they identify you as a producer and keep outdoor clothes away from food.

Other than that, looking back, I think we didn't do too badly. I just wish I could have been there back then with what I know now. We would have aced it.

Chapter 5 – Running your Business

Once you have your first event out of the way you are officially one of us. Not that you weren't before, but there are hundreds of people out there intending to start a street food business at some stage, an most never get further than the dinner party discussion or related book purchase. If you have actually traded then that's the first street food trophy. Time to think about the next one: let me assemble the full case for you.

The Street Food Trophy Case

1st	first ever event	first positive comment	first repeat customer	first actual queue	first music festival
2nd	first regular event	first blog review	first mention in regional publication	having your first £1000 day	getting staff in
3rd	Glastonbury	win an award	be recognised within the industry	selling 1000 units in a day	quit full time job
4th	featured article in a national publication	TV appearance	celebrity endorsement	getting a second unit	bricks and mortar

I think within a small tinkering margin this is what most of us hope to get from our businesses. The one about Glastonbury is a sticking point, because if you do festivals this is the first question everyone asks you. Perhaps consider doing it once, just so that you can say you have. We have turned it down because the pitch fees were too high and it's a colossal financial risk, as you have no control over your pitch, the weather or what the guys on either side will be selling. Get it right though, and you could set yourself up for months.

The trophy order is not in years or months, it's to suggest that you don't have to do everything at once. Aim for the stuff in the first tier before you start on the second, although if the opportunity presents itself, grab it with both hands.

Public Event types

There are lots of different places to trade. As more and more of us start hitting the streets and people start to trust the food we serve, this will only improve. Not only do you have the locations that were previously the preserve of our street food forefathers, the mobile caterers and festival food traders of this earth, you have all the new events that only street fooders can trade at. Making the most of this flexibility will mean you have a nice full calendar and can quit the boring full time job sooner.

Markets (Weekly)

This would have previously been the moblier's haunt. Towns which have a regular market will increasingly want street food rather than the grotty burger. Unless you are in a trendy part of London the average spend here won't be high, because these folks want a bargain and a bacon butty, but times are changing, so keep an eye out. They are usually either run directly by the local council or by a local market provider. In either case they will be well established and have their own regular traders, so they will make you work for it. The only exception to this is if the market is struggling, and then you will get it easily. Don't sign up for the whole season until you have tried it once or twice.

Markets (Speciality and Farmers)

This is much more of a street food crowd than the local market. The spend is higher and people are there specifically for nice food. The down side is that these markets are mostly at the weekend, which means that you will get other bookings in their place and will struggle to build a regular following unless you are prepared to turn down other, possibly more lucrative work.

The application process will be similar to the weekly markets, and the same warning applies: don't sign up for more than one until you have tried it.

Markets (Street Food)

This is a whole new type of market, catering specifically to the midweek lunch crowd in densely officed areas and the food enthusiasts who will travel in at the weekend. These markets may well be organised by the same folks as the ones above, and may also include producers, but expect a short, sharp burst of trade between 12 and 2, then pack up and head home. The draw here is the street food, so the offering is key. Traders with an interesting food type will get in here far more easily than mainstream traders.

Your most likely problem: If the organiser is filling gaps with low quality food. When faced with a grotty burger or no pitch fees, you can forgive them for taking whatever they can get.

Street Food Events

These are another new invention of the street food industry, another one perfect for innovative food types. It's an evening-into-night event where people come for the food and stay for the vibes and the music. You will usually find the most food-literate crowd here, so experimentation and edgy dishes will sell better than in many other places. They will often be organised by a local collective or a keen promoter, so knowing other folks in the street food scene is key to finding the best ones. Here more than anywhere, it will be your new and interesting food is what will get you trading there. They will probably have their fill of burgers.

Music Festivals

While the street food stuff keeps us ticking along, it is at music festivals that we make the majority of our money. Glastonbury is the biggest, with thousands of applications every year, but like Reading, Leeds, Download, T in the Park and V they are a logistical nightmare.

The pitch fees charged are very high, because potential earnings are colossal. On the other hand, it means that risk is colossal as well. If you get an offer think carefully about how many portions you need to take in order to cover pitch fees, then cover costs, then pay your staff and finally to actually make a sensible profit. Then consider how you would store and prepare the raw ingredients. Like I said: a logistical nightmare.

On the other hand, if you are prepared for it, you can make a substantial pile of money.

Smaller festivals, especially the kind that refer to themselves as "boutique", are often much nicer places for street food. The pitch fees are more reasonable, meaning that you can get into profit faster and start enjoying the weekend rather than just firing food out of the hatch without stopping for breath. Demand for quality food is increasing at festivals. Patrons are no longer satisfied with whatever the hell used to get served there, so these days even the big caterers and festivals are starting to look for more street food talent.

Here the fancy unit will impress, and the unique offering will secure the pitch. You will have exclusivity on your product in at least that area of the festival, and when considering two different traders offering a similar product, the one with the best looking unit will get in. Unless you have traded there before, in which case, unless you set fire to the organiser, poisoned half the guests and ran off with the money from the bar, you're probably in.

You may want to reconsider your food offering a little for music festivals. You will be stuck there for the entire weekend, away from all your regular suppliers and usually without the option to drive up to your unit to restock. At the biggest festivals this is not always the case – there will probably be a wholesaler on site, but at small to medium ones (5000-50,000) you need to take everything with you or convince a local supplier to drop it off. That may not be possible, so talk to the festival organiser.

This means that if you get fresh bread daily, you will probably need to accept that the bread will be stale and toast it, find a supplier who can deliver to site or get different buns for that festival. The same applies to fresh meat.

Plan to be on site for the entire weekend, even if you live close by, at least for the first year. Getting in and out of a festival can be incredibly time-consuming, especially if you happen to leave at the same time as the day ticket holders. The flow of guests and customers will be different between festivals, and you may discover that breakfast kicks off at sunrise and continues until 9am, so skipping home for a few hours' kip could cost you hundreds of pounds in lost revenue.

Depending on where you are within the festival you will also have different trading hours. Campsite traders are usually allowed to open 24 hours a day, with breakfast as the biggest meal. Traders in the main arena will hold the same hours as the main arena itself, meaning that you will stop when the customers get scooped back into the campsite – it can be a blessing.

Festivals are not for the faint-hearted. You will be standing in your unit, and only in your unit, for 12-17 hours a day. Your whole world becomes a tiny little bubble of (in our case) toasties and change. If things go well you will find yourself wishing these idiotic, drunk morons could just leave you be for five minutes while you have a quick tidy and a drink. Until you count the cash at the end of the day. If it's going badly you will hate the universe, the organisers, yourself and everyone nearby for shunning you. The end of day count then just serves as a reminder of how badly you have failed.

Surviving Music Festivals
It warrants a small aside: There are a few things you probably didn't know about trading at music festivals.

- You will camp next to, behind (or even inside) your unit. This is a good thing. Remember that by the end of the weekend you will hopefully have several thousand pounds of cash, which you won't want to either leave unattended or trail across site each night.
- Be paranoid about that cash. People are actively trying to steal it.
- You will crave fruit & veg by day 2. I'd recommend ambient temperature stored fruit juice.
- Take ear plugs and eye masks. If your unit happens to be in the late night party lounge, you won't sleep until they do. They don't.
- Take wellies. You will need them. Maybe not this time, but it will rain eventually.
- You, uniquely, will have power. Unlike the average festival-goer. This magical substance allows you to charge phones, pump up air beds and have lights at night. It's terribly civilised.
- You will also have hot water. You can totally take a hot water bottle as well. Unless it's July/August the nights will be cold.
- If you trade from a gazebo, you have to have a floor covering. A tarpaulin is sufficient, but long-term you will probably want to invest in something more solid.

Food Festivals (Paid)

I am not a huge fan of the paid food festival, because I think making people pay entry to then pay for food is an exceptionally clever business plan, but only if you can make it work. When it goes wrong, all too often it's the traders who lose out, because we have already paid for the pitch and are relying on people to show up.

There are good paid food festivals out there though, so don't start dispatching bags of poo to organiser's offices just yet. If you are thinking of getting involved with one, make sure you have clear estimates, in writing, of how many people will come through the door. Ideally, you want the organisers to sign a contract guaranteeing a certain number of visitors, but here's the thing: they will be the ones doing the counting on the gate.

These events are characterised by fairly high pitch fees, heavy competition and huge susceptibility to the rain if they are held in summer. We visit an October one and the provision for rain is excellent, meaning that naturally, it never rains. People normally decide to visit these events on the day, based on the weather, rather than buying tickets months in advance like a music festival, so if it rains it will be a ghost town.

Food Festivals (Free)

These run in much the same way as paid for festivals, but generally speaking they are held in town centres rather than out-of-town destination venues. This means there will usually be at least basic passing trade, and anyone who notices the event will come for a wander round.

The same problems with paid for food festivals will occur, so you will still get comparatively high pitch fees, lots of competition and a ghost town in the rain, but people will be more willing to part with money for hot food, rather than trying to fill up on free samples. Although don't get me wrong, that will totally happen as well.

The key to picking a good food festival is to go for the established ones. New ones are popping up everywhere, and often offering fairly cheap fees to come and trade, but be wary of first time events. Check out their online promotion and if you live nearby, keep an eye out for any posters or news articles. If you don't know about it, how will anyone else?

Historical Re-enactments

Like music festivals, this is another one where we trade alongside the festival caterers.

These events are great fun, and well worth applying to if you have gaps to fill. In many cases they are run by the council, English Heritage and the National Trust, charities or period re-enactment groups. We have so far found that this results in much more reasonable pitch fees than music festivals of comparative size, and generally less competition for hot food.

Plus you can see knights and spitfires and Vikings, and who doesn't love a good bit of history some times?

If you have the site of a famous battle in your area, the chances are someone puts on an annual re-enactment of whatever happened there, and that may be a good place to start. This is a pretty close-knit community though, and because the events are good the same caterers will keep going back. Be persistent, and don't be put off by a rejection in your first year. Keep coming back, keep improving your offering and be sure to emphasize how wonderfully local you are (if applicable, that is).

County Shows

The pitch fees can be astronomical here, because the catering has always been provided by dedicated festival caterers who can bosh out burger+bun in seconds. The footfall though, means that these events are occasionally worth the money, but I would approach with caution: County shows are quite specifically about doing things the good old fashioned way, so the really aren't too bothered about street food yet.

In a lot of cases though, you will find the main stumbling block is because they are held at show grounds which already have their own on-site catering. Unless you sign up to an entire year (usually tendered) you simply won't get a look in.

Car/VW/Steam/Balloon Shows

We can lump all these under the general category of shows for enthusiasts. Obviously if you trade from a car, VW, steam vehicle or hot air balloon you may well have an advantage here, but again, as with the country shows, they are usually held at a showground, meaning dedicated catering.

In some cases though they will be organises by very enthusiastic amateurs, who, to be blunt, may not know how much to charge for a food concession. You can get some very good deals here, so it's worth keeping your eyes peeled. On the flip side of that, enthusiastic amateurs may not have the foggiest idea how to market or promote an event. As with all things, established events are much safer than new ones.

Charity Events
These are family events most of the time, with a lovely crowd and some very passionate supporters. They're also great for building a local following if you can't get in on a market nearby.

Charity events are complicated from a business point of view, even though of course they are great for giving back to society. You are, first and foremost, a business. This means that you need to make money to be successful, and charity events are all about making money for a good cause. Be clear with the organiser up front about how much they are expecting you to contribute. If you have the time and inclination to help with the fundraising then that's fab, they will be delighted, but if you need to view this as purely a business opportunity be open about it.

This kind of event is frequently organised by local clubs or volunteers, who will devote hours of time into getting it off the ground. Booking you to come and trade occasionally carries the implication that you will also join the committee and attend the meetings, so figuring this out early really helps.

If you are approached after the event and asked for a donation that you had not agreed in advance then remember you are not obliged to provide one, nor is it ok for them to guilt-trip you into it. Again, giving back to society is great, but "The funds have already been allocated elsewhere, sorry" is a useful way to say no without causing offence.

As an added incentive to donate: pitch fees paid for a charity event are actually a "charitable donation" and can be offset against taxes (ask your accountant for details). Double-check with the organiser that this is actually the case though; you may be working for a company on behalf of a charity.

Sports events

Cross-country runs, cycle rides and hard core endurance races are just so fashionable right now. There will often be a few hundred people on site including participants and spectators, which is usually enough to support a hot food and a coffee van. Trade here will come in waves, so as each group of runners set off you get a burst of sales, and again as they return. It's not going to set you up for retirement, because these people are here to do exercise and get fit, not to indulge in your delicious dining options, so don't expect terribly strong trade.

This sort of event should be either low pitch fee or no pitch fee for you – if you are really not sure, for example if they are not clear on numbers, don't be afraid to charge up front, you might otherwise end up standing there doing nothing for no money all day.

The Permanent Pitch

This is something many first-time street food traders think will be their goal, because that's what most people see most regularly. We've all seen the jacket potato guy in town do a roaring trade over lunch, and it seems like a nice steady source of income.

Depending on how you choose to run your business, it may or may not be for you. It's a big commitment, getting your license off the council and then showing up, regular as clockwork, every single day no matter the weather.

You will rely on repeat custom, and the terms of the license may also prevent you from taking random days off when you don't fancy it. This will rule you out of festivals in summer and mean you will potentially have to work a 7 day week to pack in profitable weekend events as well. You may realise that actually, you only make £50 a day for your troubles, and you are bored out of your mind for 4.5 of the 6 hours you spend there.

We have never really fancied the permanent pitch, because variety is what makes this job so much fun. We still tried to get one in

Leamington Spa, way back in the day, and failed most efficiently. If you do think that a permanent pitch might be the way forward for you, you need a street trading license from the council. Once you have that, depending on the council, you will either need an approved pitch (which you have to find and get them to approve) or you need to be in a county that has designated consent streets.

These are places where you can rock up and trade from, as long as you are not obstructing traffic or causing trouble. Think laybys on A-roads or carparks on industrial estates. You need to find footfall, and then work on getting approval to trade there. Often you will be met with a very concise "no" from the council, but don't be put off. Times are changing and if you put the effort in, really show them that you would add to the area, you may eventually get somewhere.

Private Hire

These events are great if you do a fairly common food type. Hog roasts, pizzas, burgers and hotdogs will all find great demand for their services, especially in the wedding season.

Methods vary, but most private hire is paid for in advance and then served on the night. This means you are not paying pitch fees, so the profit here is significantly higher than at any other kind of street food event, even though the portion numbers will not be massive – weddings of more than 150 are reasonably rare. The downside is that almost every single event of this manner happens on a Saturday night in summer, so you have a very finite number of potential booking days. Often they are also booked by the happy couple, who want everything just so. We have email chains 30 mails long for some weddings. Financially you are swapping the pitch fee for a time investment.

Make sure you set out exactly what services you are going to provide and how you are going to do it. Being clear with your customer will avoid a whole minefield of problems later.

I'll cover the main types of events and the things you need to be aware of with each. As these are booked by the customer approaching you, this is work you will get through word of mouth or via the website rather than work you can tender for. This is when a well optimised, search-engine-friendly website will actually make you money.

A strong social media presence is essential here. You want these people to part with money up-front, so they need to know that you actually exist, and won't vaporize the moment their cheque has cleared. They will do their research, so make sure you have something for them to find.

Weddings

Street food is now a legitimate evening food option at weddings. It's simpler and much, much cheaper than getting a buffet in. We can do hot, crowd-pleasing food without any hassle at all, because we come with all our own kit, without any of the clean-up.

Make sure you clarify a few things in advance:

- **Agree how many portions you will bring.** If you have a menu with multiple options, agree how many of each option will be available on the night. This means that you are covered if somehow the meat option runs out half way through. Your average bride and groom will probably not have organised their own wedding food before, so providing guidance on portions and numbers will be appreciated.
- **Agree when and how payment is due.** Usually a deposit to secure the date, paid in advance, and then the balance settled closer to the time. We do 50% to secure the date and then 50% no less than a week before the event. If this is not an option you may want to settle the balance in cash on the night instead, or invoice them afterwards. I wouldn't recommend the invoice afterwards; it can become hard work very quickly, especially if something goes wrong on the night, but if you are just starting out it may be a good way to show willing.
- **Agree serving times.** Especially if there is still food left, it's very hard to leave. Agreeing a set serving time means they will not expect you to hang around all night, which otherwise they probably will – they paid for the food, after all. Remember that your time is included in that price. A three hour serving window is plenty, providing you can make enough portions in that time. We usually recommend 8-11pm.

- **Agree what happens with any remaining, uneaten food.** We offer to stay on at a fixed rate per hour, payable on the night in cash. We tell them about this up front in writing so that there is no confusion or embarrassment on the night. If they would rather not spend the extra (most don't) then we cook off what's left (or a proportion of it) and leave it on the side indoors somewhere.
- **Agree a wet weather provision**. If it's a wedding in the off-season this is especially important. You can't be running table service all night, so bringing food in to people directly isn't an option. Instead you can either make it clear that you need to be parked right outside the doors, or offer to bring your own shelter, or bring in trays of cooked food and leave them in a designated area.
- **Bring something that kids will eat**. We very strongly recommend that the ham & cheese toastie makes an appearance at every wedding. Otherwise we will spend the entire night butchering much tastier toasties into something children will tolerate. Even then, we still bring a tray of plain cheese and plain ham toasties as well.
- **Check dietary requirements**. If you can provide a gluten free/veggie/dairy free option then it's worth checking this. If you are meat-in-a-bun, no frills, then make sure they are not expecting anything beyond that.

I would recommend an email in the final week before the wedding in which you spell out all this again, even if it has been previously discussed. This also gives them a prompt to give you the final change of heart on the menu, which is easy a week in advance, but will be a right pain 24 hours before the event. Make sure you have details of exactly when you will be arriving, the location and post code of the venue, a contact number of someone you can call on the day if things go pear-shaped (the best man or maid of honour) and details of any dietary requirements they have requested (including that they haven't requested any).

This should cover both parties against any eventuality and give you something to reference on the day when you are already on the road and realise you don't know where you're going.

Corporate Events

My personal favourite in the private hire sector, these are the gigs you want to get involved with. No pitch fees and payment in advance, but the potential of regular income as well and often glorious midweek trade. Here the website is crucial. You will often be booked by someone's PA or secretary, so they will google local food trucks, and that's where you want to be.

While weddings will tend to shop around and then pick the one that looks like the best deal for them, corporate clients tend to pick the one that is easiest. Throwing pictures and health and safety documentation in the first email (Public liability, food hygiene, gas & PAT certificate, risk assessment) means that they don't then have to chase you for them, you probably know what you're doing and are less likely to screw up on the day. Try and take the work out of the event, so propose a menu, arrival and serving times and specify your electricity needs right there in the first email (if you have enough info to do so) so all they have to do is throw a bit of money at you.

Non-Wedding Family Events

These are all the other family occasions: 21st birthdays, christenings, funerals and everything else in between. I confess, we've not done a funeral yet, but it is, quite literally, only a matter of time.

The same rules as weddings apply here, but you don't run the risk of ruining the best day of someone's life, so the ante isn't quite as high. There will probably be a lot of kids around though, especially at christenings and children's parties. When planning the menu with the customer, make sure you have an accessible "kids" option on. We will generally end up taking a tray of ham toasties and a tray of cheese toasties alongside the ham and cheese, because it's just more efficient than pulling one or the other out each time a kid wants to eat.

Sports Events

These are similar to events where you pay them pitch fees, but on a smaller scale. If you are unsure about numbers then it's not unreasonable to charge the organiser for you to show up. It falls somewhere between the private hire and public event model, but it's a good way to make a smaller event worth your while. If they only need a food van for the 30-50 hungry people who *might* want to eat there is no point in you showing up. On the other hand, if you charge a nominal fee to cover your food and staff costs for the day, then suddenly everything you take is profit. If you can then take food that will happily keep until the following day then even if you serve nothing at all you have still made a profit.

Sports events, especially charity ones, are unique because they also use a great deal of volunteers. These folks give up their precious time for the good of the event, and can usually expect a meal in return. Offering a reduced rate, pre-paid menu for these guys is a great way of adding extra income to an event.

Obviously this is not a business model that works for everyone, because those of you who would not be able to roll stock forward would struggle, but we have made good money here in the past, and even on bad days at least the risk is fairly low.

Other Events
There are loads of opportunities out there for the taking, most of which will probably come with their own set of problems. The most important thing is to tell your prospective client exactly what they are going to get for their money. It can save you a world of pain later on and makes you look much more reputable to the event organiser. I'll cover how you work out what to charge for your services further into the chapter.

Making Festival Organisers Love You
There is no magic bullet here, because festival organisers are a motley pack of folks who come from every single background imaginable, and are all looking for slightly different things. However if you know what they are looking for, it might help you get those first few events, take the pictures and build your experience.

Simplicity
They want it to be easy; above almost everything else - Except money. I mention this first though; this is something you have control over. Prompt responses, detailed but concise applications and the ability to send all the paperwork in one go will actually make you

stand out. When you show up on the day, find them and ask all your questions in one go, rather than hunting out different staff members throughout the day.

Variety

They can only have one of each type of food at their festival (although sometimes there will be multiple arenas with a certain amount of overlap), so out of the 15 burger applications, they will only take one or two. Serve something different, and they can book you straight in. Serve it from an interesting unit and they will be falling over themselves to have you.

Money

Paying promptly once the event is agreed and you are booked in not only gives you security for that weekend, it gives them one less thing to think about. This shouldn't mean you just blindly accept the number they quote, but once you do have a number, pay it within their deadlines. Just for the love of toast do you research on them first and make sure they are an actual business, have an actual festival, and are selling you a pitch they actually own. Members of NCASS can check with in with head office for details if you're not sure. Non-members need to put in the research or risk being royally screwed over.

Being Nice

It sounds obvious, but a lot of these people are just doing their job. They are not getting a share of the profits and they are just coming to work. If you remember their name, chat about the good times and compliment them on a job well done, or complain in a manner that is factual rather than angry, they would rather have you back next year than the guy who went ape because there was a 30 second power outage.

Spotting a Good or Bad Event

This is one of those invaluable skills that comes with a medal and a little certificate that proclaims you the winner of street food generally. I start with a disclaimer: there is no way anyone can definitively predict what will be a good event. Not you, not the organiser and not even the customer, who is the one with the final word on the matter.

A great event is the one the organiser has poured their heart and soul into, has invested a pot of cash in and, to a certain extent, has got lucky on. Spotting these events (or their distant but weirdly similar looking cousin, the dreadful event) is 50% experience, 50% luck. Anything that can sway the odds a tiny bit in your favour here is a good thing.

These symptoms are observed, not scientifically established, and individually don't mean anything at all. If you observe lots of them though, you will see a pattern forming.

The Bad Event	The Good Event
Approaches you. They can't find anyone else.	Won't even answer your emails because their traders keep coming back
Seems disorganised – they don't ask for documentation.	Is asking for all the documents up front.
May ask you to help with promotion	Is sold out already, or mostly sold out.
Will be vague, evasive or even refuse to give you details on ticket sales.	Will be happy to brag about last year, tickets sold or pre sales.
Won't put anything in writing	Will get you to sign a contract (read it!)
It's their first time. Huge risk here.	Has been going for years. Established events are much more secure.
Asks for pitch fees well in advance	Is happy to settle for a percentage.
Changes the terms of the	Is happy to discuss exactly

agreement after you have paid.	what they want you to do
You found them in an online backwater and they fill an otherwise dead weekend.	You have already heard of them before you started out in street food.
Long travel times.	Is local to you: you get regular repeat custom.
Is evasive over the number of traders.	The anticipated ratio of traders to patrons is good.
Quiet on social media, very few followers, no discernible promotion. Interactions are all from the same three people.	Is all over social media – crucially - getting interaction from followers and palpable excitement for the event.

In summary, you need to ask questions. They don't have to be invasive, but there may well be a lot of your money on the line, so don't be afraid to ask. If they won't or don't answer you should hear the sound of alarm bells, klaxons and reverse light warnings going off all around you.

They might just give up and offer the pitch to someone else if you get too inquisitive. This sucks, but it might just save your skin from a bad event. Do you really want to give hundreds (thousands) of pounds to someone who can't reliably tell you how many caterers they are planning to have on site? Move on, but keep half an eye on their facebook page. If the event turns out to be terrible/amazing, this is where customers will share that useful information with the world. There's always next year.

You also need to know that these things are not all black and white. With the best will in the world, sometimes it just doesn't work out. Everything can look perfect, and then you show up on the day and it's awful. But there are almost always warning signs. You can choose to ignore them, you can put a brave face on things and you can stick by the event, but you are better off doing your research and getting out before it's too late.

I speak from bitter experience here, and I expect you will need to learn this the hard way too, because you want to believe. Honestly, it's like an obsession. You want this festival, they accept you, and you are so delighted you ignore the common sense voice that is patiently explaining why it will be a money-sink.

It is impossible to get your money back afterwards. If you had a bad event, chances are the event organiser did as well, and will be hanging on to every single penny. You can complain, you can stamp your feet, but once the money has left your bank account nothing short of a lawsuit will get it back. This is why having things in writing is so important, because a legal case is built on facts. If they told you there would be 5 caterers and you get there to find 10, that's misrepresentation – you may have something. If they said they *expected* 3000 people and only 2 men and a sheep show up, you have squat, because they just happened to be wrong.

Please do complain. Tell other traders, tell NCASS and voice your concerns loud and clear to the organiser. The only way we will ever get change in this industry is if we don't just sit by silently.

NCASS will provide free legal advice if you're a member, and you can always get together with other caterers to build a joint lawsuit. In the long run though, you are better set avoiding this kind of problem in advance rather than planning to fight it through the courts after the event.

In summary: If you want to do music festivals or big events, you need to have enough in the bank to be able to offset at least one annual horrific event.

Making the Numbers Work

Accountancy is one thing, but you need the money coming in before you start worrying about who will manage it for you. That means making stock + time = money. Shouldn't be too hard. Here we go.

Private Hire Costing

The easiest way to charge for your services when paid for in advance is to agree a certain number of portions at a certain pric You can then include your time, you staff, a mileage charge and a other sundries you think you can get away with.

Most private hire events will probably be for 50-150 people, meaning that at the bottom end, you probably won't be making enough money for it to be worth your while getting out of bed. In that situation decide on a minimum call out charge, to make sure it's worth your while. We charge less for midweek events than weekend ones, but that's entirely up to you. You need to work out how much you would be aiming to make on an average Saturday, and that's the amount your private hire gig needs to spend. Otherwise you might as well save yourself the trouble.

If they want you to come out and sell to their guests, but only have 50 guests there, you can also charge a call-out fee. This method can work brilliantly for both parties: They pay £100 and their guests are fed, you get £100 for free and still sell a nice amount of food. To work out how many portions you will probably sell you need to know how long the event is on for, how many meal times are covered and whether there is any food provided.

Assuming the event starts between 6-8pm guests will be hungry, maybe won't have eaten dinner. You can expect to serve most of them as long as there is no other food provided. If you are there to cover an afternoon, say 2-5pm, you are sitting after lunch and before dinner. You will be lucky to even see a quarter of them. We also use the portion equation for a more scientific sounding quote. See below.

Portion Calculations

In a perfect world, at the end of each event, you will have one portion left of each of the items you sell. Why one? Simple: if you sell out, there is the possibility you could have sold more. What if an extra 5 portions would all have shifted? That's an extra £20- £30 you could have made. So having one left is the best case scenario. Just to give you an idea: since we started trading in 2011 it's happened to us maybe 4 times.

That's a perfect event. No wastage, no missed sales.

Forget those for now. Instead you need to work out how to minimise your wastage. Maximising sales we'll deal with elsewhere. This means taking the right number of portions for the event in question. These are the three methods we use for working that out:

1: A percentage of pitch fees.

Generally, you will be paying up front for the events and then trying to get your money's-worth on the day. This means aiming to have the pitch fees at 10-20%. So at a market where the fees are £100 you want to be taking home between £500 and £1000. If you are a gourmet burger person with high ingredient costs then you aim for the top end, if you are a pancake person with low ingredient costs you aim for the other. The rest of us slot in between.

Anything over 25% starts to become bad value very quickly, so you should always expect to do 20%. This means that at a market you are unfamiliar with, on your first outing, you can reasonably aim for 20% pitch fees. Bring on the example!

Pitch fees are £60, you are a quinoa-dog-on-a-stick seller with a price point of £5. You are visiting the Poshington-on-Thames Saturday Food Gallery for the first time. So you aim for 20% pitch fees. This means you are expecting to earn £300, so you will need to take 60 portions.

What with Poshington being full of ultra-hip ex-Londoners you should easily be able to shift those 60. If you sell out you can then bring more next time, safe in the knowledge that you didn't pay too much for your pitch. If you don't sell out then you know that those lumberjack shirt & trilby hatted 20-somethings may not be the right crowd for you.

The dream is to find a market that really works for your food and brand, where you can get the percentage right down. This takes time, but if your product is good, you can potentially do it anywhere. The trick is to notice whether a market is on the up or not. Talking to other traders is a great help here.

The percentage method works well for small or one day events, but won't help you at all on multiday or tendered pitches. For that you will need the patented Jabberwocky Portion Equation.

2: *The Portion Equation*

For big events it's worth getting some numbers off the organiser. Ask them how many caterers they will be getting (c) and how many guests they are expecting (g). Then work out how many meal times you will be on site for (m). With most weekend festivals this will be 7 (Friday dinner, and then breakfast, lunch and dinner Saturday and Sunday, but make sure you check, it will make a difference). At any given meal time, only half of the people on site will eat.

There is one further variable that you will need to know, and it's a tricky one. It's how popular you are in relation to the other caterers on site. It's a number between 0 and about 3. If you are a celebrity chef, a chain restaurant or have TV cameras following you then you score much higher, but otherwise the values of the main foods are (very much approximately) as follows:

1.5 – Burgers

1.4 – Hogroast

1.3 – Sausage

1.2 – Hotdogs

1.1 - Chips

1.0 – Pizza

1.0 – Paella

0.9 – Familiar World Food (Thai, Curry, Chinese)

0.8 – Burritos/Mexican

0.7 – Other, unfamiliar meat-based food

0.6 – Vegetarian / Vegan

0.5 – Dessert

We call it the popularity index, or (PI). You could shorten it to (x). You could even call it your (x) factor. But seriously, have a little self-respect.

These numbers are highly situational, and really shouldn't be taken as gospel, because all sorts of factors can affect them. If the veggie guy is in a prime location serving from a huge and beautiful unit, he will do better than the burger guy selling manky-looking burgers from a white trailer round the back, but all other factors aside, these numbers should give you somewhere to start.

You then need to assemble your equation as follows:

Guests (g) multiplied by mealtimes (m) multiplied by your Popularity Index (PI), divided by 2 (the half of your customer base who won't eat at that meal) times your caterers (c).

This looks mathematically a little like this:

$$n = \frac{m\,PI\,g}{2c}$$

An example for your troubles:

The Summer Stick Weekender have offered you a pitch. You make your enquiries and are informed that they expect between 3000 and 4000 people through the gates, last year they had a sell-out of 4000 people. It's an established weekend of camping with fun, frolics and poking things with sticks featuring 7 hot food caterers, including you. You have been accepted for your exciting jambalaya dumplings.

To start with, you look at the numbers the organiser gives you and work out if they are probable, or guess-work. Stick Fest is an established event, and last year was a sell-out, so you can expect more of the same, and chances are these estimates are probable. If it's a new event, or numbers have been significantly increased from last year, then you may want to take the lower end of their estimate, and possibly halve it. If it's a brand new event the organiser will have no idea how many people might turn up, so expect anywhere between 0 and 10,000. This is why new events are risky.

With that in mind, you assemble your maths. You are selling unfamiliar meat-based food with 6 mealtimes, as there's no music after 6 pm on Sunday. Your formula looks like this:

m=6   PI=0.7   g=4000   c=7

$$\frac{6 \times 0.7 \times 4000}{2 \times 7} = 1200$$

1200 Portions. That's how many you can work on selling over the whole weekend. It's really not an exact science, but that should give you something to go on. At a tendered event you can now offer 10-20% (depending on how badly you want it) of the money you would earn if you sold that many, and be reassured that maths is on your side. If you are paying pitch fees it's worth then calculating the percentages, to see if you can hit 10-20%. If you do, then you are provisionally onto a winner.

Using this for costing a private hire where patrons buy their own food is also a nice way to back up your numbers. Calculate the portions you should sell, and then charge the customer whatever the difference is between that and your minimum call out charge:

A private hire 30th birthday party, guests will be paying for their own food. It's a Saturday night and there will be 50 of them. Your minimum call out charge is £400. You can expect to sell 25 portions of your salmon bagel burgers as your PI is about 1 when you trade alone. You charge £6.50, so that will make you £162.50. Subtract that from your call out charge and the customer can purchase your services for £237.50.

3. *The Repeat Event*
This is the easy one. You have traded there before, and you sold 100 units. Chances are that if you trade there again, providing the weather is the same and the guy next to you isn't doing your exact food, you will also sell 100 units. Take whatever you sold last time. If you sold out, add an extra 10-15 for next time.

Pitch Fees

This is the upfront cash that you give the organiser for the pleasure and permission of trading at their event. It does not include a table, a gazebo or any sort of equipment – except at markets, where you will usually get a waterproof stall and a 2-3m table.

In most cases though, you are paying for some square meterage of ground space on a particular day. The most common method is to pay pitch fees when you are confirmed on the event. This will be a few weeks ahead with markets, a few months ahead with food festivals and at the start of the season for music festivals. If you are planning on having a summer of festival-hopping, portaloo surveying and tent-sleeping, you will be paying for it between February and April.

As with many things in street food, pitch fees are not set in stone. Especially with big festivals there will usually be some wiggle room, so don't be afraid to haggle. Especially armed with your Portions Equation, you can demonstrate that they are asking for too much and might be able to lever the price down. They might also just stop answering your emails and find someone else. It's a delicate balance.

Tendering for a Pitch

I touched on this above, but it's an annoying pastime, so it probably deserves a little more space. Tendering is when the organisers offer you a provisional pitch, then ask you to offer them enough money to make it worth their while. As someone who has probably never traded there before, you do not have the faintest idea how to make it worth their while, much less whether it will subsequently be worth your while.

Bear in mind that once you have reached this stage, they are probably quite keen to have you. This works in your favour. If you are an obscure food seller, rejoice, you are probably the only one they have, and they will accept a lower tender. Burger, pizza and sausage people need to tender higher to get in, because the festival will probably have had a lot of applications from those types of food, and you will also make more money.

First, you need to get the basic details about the event: how many guests each day (or for the weekend, if it's a mostly camping event) and how many other caterers. Then plug that into the Portion

142

Equation as explained earlier. That should give you your first number. To cross-reference that, as you would normally with the pitch fees, you need to have a busy day on your books.

Hark back to the last time you were reasonably busy. Not running at full capacity, just fairly busy, all day long. Use that as a reference to calculate how much you could make over the weekend. Assume that the festival will be around that good, and see how it compares to the numbers provided by the portion equation. If you have a match, tender 10-20%.

They will probably haggle. You can too.

Trading Locally

It happened to us by accident; a happy circumstance caused by having an unreliable van, but local trading is one of the things that saved us in our first couple of years. Not only does it make breakdowns less of a pain, it reduces travelling time and costs, and gives you that most glorious of customers: the repeat buyer.

It's worth concentrating your search locally. If you are London-based you will be looking to secure a regular pitch on the same market each day of the week, but for the rest of us it means finding a few markets locally, and then concentrating on one area nearby for trade. If you live near a big population hub you're in luck, and it's worth focussing your efforts up there, but don't underestimate the local market.

We trade in Leamington as much as we possibly can. It's a mile from our house, and there are enough events dotted throughout the year for us to be a recognisable fixture in the town centre. Any events we put out on twitter will result in a few groups of regulars swinging down to grab food. So it's worth us going to every event there, because they all work out better. Leamington remains the only place where we stand a fighting chance of outselling the burger or pizza person, which is always quietly satisfying.

Even if you're rural it's worth picking a local town and trying to secure all the events they do. On a quiet day it can make all the difference.

Secondary Speciality

Assuming you are brave, and make the choice to live a life less ordinary with a food that isn't meat-in-a-bun, you may find that while it gets you into all sorts of markets and festivals, the private bookings seem a little slow. Street food is still a novelty at weddings, so people tend to want to play it safe, and a hog roast is good and safe.

We have the added bonus of a cool van, which makes us desirable at weddings, but only the brave will go for the toastie menu. Most people will tentatively enquire about almost any food other than toasties. So we offer pulled pork as well. Once they have enquired we usually end up selling them the toastie menu, but that's beside the point. If you are hoping for wedding trade it's probably worth considering a main-stream alternative, but try to stick to your guns out at markets. Remember why you chose honey-glazed chick-pea skewers and keep at it, the food world will be a better place for your diligence.

Weekend vs. Weekday Trading

When you first start out, I expect it will be like us, with a full time job midweek and a market at the weekend. This can go on to provide a nice little cash bonus, but doesn't get you out of the rat race. When you do eventually quit, you will probably need to jump right into midweek trade to keep your earnings high enough, and that can be a bit of a shock.

Midweek trade has far fewer people. Granted, you could probably have guessed that. But then they also don't seem to want lunch. Fair enough, you're probably going to have sandwiches from home some times.

144

Then they actually do start taking an interest in your menu, but lament how expensive you food is. Unbelievable. Sadly, midweek trade just isn't as bountiful as the stuff at the weekend. People are more likely to have a set budget, less likely to be feeling adventurous and probably in a hurry.

Midweek retail markets are a classic example of this. If you can find a farmers market you might have more luck, but they are usually still not great. You will be able to make a living if you can hit a retail every day, establish your business and get a solid local following, but you will have to put the work in.

A combination of weekday and weekend events is the most common strategy for full timers. Visit and trade at all the local midweek activities, and then keep the ones that work for you. Weekend events you should be aiming higher. Pitch fees will start to soar, so making a market work becomes a lot more urgent. Either run with a few weekend markets, commit to them and make them work, or mix things up and go for variety.

If there is enough trade locally then you might find that the steady, reasonably predictable income from a pair of regular weekend markets is better value than hunting for and applying to thousands of festivals, but while it is a more solid strategy if you are planning to expand your business, because you have a nice secure starting point, you won't have the big pots of cash that can be amassed at food and music festivals.

In Summary

It's all about finding what works for your food type. There are so many different ways to trade that you can make anything work as long as you put the effort in, but you want to be doing what you love, as that's what makes street food fun.

Chapter 6 – Long Term

Congratulations! You have survived your first few events, established that street food is the thing for you and now you want to make a living out of it. This means using your time as efficiently as possible to make the most of the weeks and months that seem to slip by without you having a chance to notice them. There are some fine points to all this, but basically, you need to maximise profit.

Maximising Profit

A friend of mine once said that turnover is for showoffs, and he's right. An annual turnover of £120,000 with a net profit of £20,000 is much, much worse than turnover of £80,000 with a profit of £18,000. You are working an extra 50% for a measly 2k in the bank. Don't even get me started on VAT (I've covered it later). So now you are set up, look at each area of your business and see where you could streamline. That's not the same thing as economising or cutting corners: may my soul forever be tormented in the 7th pit of office-speak, but it's about optimisation.

Wastage

To begin with, this is where most of your profit will go. You make 200 portions, sell 150 and throw the rest away. Using the portion equation should help, but there will still be wastage. Buy a chest freezer. Work out which parts of your food can be frozen without loss off quality and which can't. If you have a whole dish which can be frozen without any deterioration then that is your go-to dish for events when you don't know how many portions you will sell.

Buy a small commercial vacuum packer. It's worth investing in a commercial one – the domestic ones are a waste of effort. Cooked meat can be stored for 4 days in the fridge, but vac-packed it goes for 10. This means, crucially, that you can get to next weekend, when you will be trading again. Non-freezable foods are quite possibly vac-packable.

There is also the matter of how much you pay for your ingredients. While I am an advocate of using local quality, there is no reason why you can't shop around. No matter where you are, there will be competition on some, if not all of your ingredients. The suppliers may be hard to find, but even a saving of a few pence can make all the difference when you are buying in bulk over long periods.

Increasing Sales

Anything that ups the number of units you sell is good. Look at your setup.

- Is it stupidly clear what you sell?
- Is there a giant board, above head-height, that proclaims, in no more than 3 words, what people can hope to find at your stall?
- Are you visible in the dark?
- Is your menu clear and easy to read?
- Is it obvious who to speak to, to place your order?
- Do you look "open"?
- Is your stall clean?
- Is your kit in good repair?
- Do you have an amusing, instagramable quote or saying plastered on a visible surface?

All of these things will probably only increase sales by a few percent each, but add them all together, and that's an extra 10% of sales, permanently, at every event from now on.

Most of those are self-explanatory or covered earlier, but let me clarify a few. If there are 4 of you standing behind the stall, even if none of you are staring at your phones or into space, the customer still has to pick a member of staff to address. Either work out who is going to grab eye-contact and greet them cheerily, or put up a sign saying "order here".

Looking open is harder, especially if you are unlit. Once you are ready to serve, especially if it's early or late, consider investing in a small sign that confirms you are ready to trade. If you have lights, turn them on. Also, never underestimate the value of a free show. People will watch almost anything. If you can move your visual cooking from the back of the stall to the front, you will get an audience.

Sticking with the Good Events
In our first year, we took every single event that we could find. For weeks on end we never got a break, but the money rolled in. In our second year, we were more cautious, only taking events that we knew could be good. By our third year, we hardly took any midweek events, and had a fair few weekends off. But we were making more money.

Once you find a good event, stick with it. It will take a few years, and you will have to go through that panicky first year where you

148

trade at every event you can find, but once you are out the other side you can be more selective. We have more time to prepare for big events, which would previously have been done between the evening of one and the morning of the next. It means that we can go for longer at the big events, because we're not wasting our time with £150 markets in the middle.

On the flip side of that, you need to be able to make a swift exit from a sinking ship. It's tempting to cling onto a poor market, because £100 is better than sitting at home doing nothing all day, but actually, unless you are in a real financial crisis, it's not. That day of trade will cost you, on average, a few hours of prep and cleaning the day before, and a totally lost day on site. You could have been hunting for new events, polishing the social media, ringing up festival organisers, doing accounts – this is the great curse of owning your own business: your work is never done.

Sourcing

I've covered sourcing in various places, but while it's an important part of street food, I would always recommend getting out there with what you can, and then refining your product as you go along. Your methods will change anyway as your business evolves, and a year down the line you will look back at those first few weeks and wonder how you could possibly have thought that pre-cooking toasties at the start of service was a good idea (it's not, but we did).

While you are trialling your menu, before you hit the great outdoors, chances are you will be using supermarket produce, possibly topped up with some regional specialities from the area in question. Once you are out there you initially exchange supermarket for market and wholesaler, and here is where you can refine.

I'd start with the thing you use most of, which will probably be either your meat or your carbs. With us, it was bread. Then work your way backwards in order of quantities used. That way the biggest improvements will be early on in your trading career, but your food will keep on improving from the customers' point of view. If they liked it last time, just wait till they try it now. This is why street food uses quality produce after all: it tastes better. There is no point in using more expensive local produce when the stuff from the wholesaler is tastier. Only one in 10 customers actually cares; the rest will only judge you on taste.

It might seem like a whole lot of effort for the 1 in 10. I agree, it is. Thankfully the taste will have the rest of them coming back, because even if they succumb to the cheap and nasty version of your food some other time, yours still tasted better. We are often told we serve the best toastie they have ever eaten. They're right, of course, but this is largely due to the fact that, even if they are making it at home, they're probably not using organic ham and artisan bread.

There are other, more subtle benefits as well. You're more likely to get featured in the media, you are a more desirable choice for private hire events and you can hold your head high if you are ever quizzed on animal welfare. You can also charge more for it. Gee whiz, I almost forgot the mention that.

You don't need to be organic free range and sourced from within 10 miles from day one, so gather suppliers gradually, and remember to check if they deliver. A few quid of delivery is much, much better value than an hour of your time + petrol to collect.

Hiring Staff

If you do need to hire staff then remember that no one will ever love your business as much as you do. You really can't expect them to; you only pay them by the hour after all.

Whether you use friends or casual staff on dreaded zero hour contracts, I would urge you to be totally clear about what you need them to do, and get everything in writing. As soon as you start hiring staff you will realise how expensive people actually are.

They also want to work fewer hours than you, take breaks (ha!) eat meals and get paid for their services, even when they definitely were not working as hard as you were *and* you made no money that day and won't be paying yourself.

This is the tough part. Throughout street food you have been paying yourself in Asda value meals and hopeful thoughts, and now someone comes along needing money. Not only do they have rights to all the things mentioned above (you don't have to provide them with free meals, but you do have to give them a chance to eat) they also have the right to minimum wage.

This is why most street food businesses are run by two business partners, both of whom are paying themselves only just enough to live on. Staff, especially in the early days, are just too expensive.

If you do need to hire then the government provides one of the only free jobs websites out there, where you can post your vacancy and be sure it will reach a large number of people. Until the government change it again, the little tinkers, you can find it here: https://www.gov.uk/jobsearch

The other option is social media, where you may even find aspiring street food folks wanting to work for free, in exchange for the work experience. Just bear in mind that they might not turn up if you're not paying them, and they have every right to just wander off if they get bored.

Giving Advice

The easy advice is when people are undecided and need a little push towards a choice, because otherwise they will be staring at your menu, blocking your queue, for many weeks to come. Asking what they are torn between usually helps.

They will quite often ask for a recommendation, which is odd, as clearly all of your food is amazing. Seeing as they ask: Pick your second most expensive dish. It looks more genuine than suggesting the most costly thing on the menu, and will probably get you the sale.

The other advice is to folks six months backwards down the line. Remember how you went sniffing around other peoples' setups before you started? Watching other folks cook similar foods and wondering if you should or could do the same? Well that's all for you to look forward to now. You will find that people ask some really quite random and at times quite invasive questions, and they always choose to do it while you're in the middle of a rush.

You don't have to tell then anything, particularly about money. We may have set ourselves up as the place to call for free street food advice, but you really shouldn't feel obliged. Just because they have bought your food doesn't mean they have the right to pick your brains on the concept, so just be delightfully vague and they'll soon get the message.

When in doubt you can always point them at our website or the book.

Negativity aside, it's great to have new people coming into street food. Folks are leaving the industry all the time, either because they couldn't make it work or because they are moving on to bigger and better things. Having new blood keeps things interesting, and means there are always new ideas floating around. We can't work on our own, so we need these people to work alongside. There is no such thing as a one man street food market, after all.

Making Bad Markets Work

This is a tricky one. There are a lot of average places to trade, and quite a few bad ones. In fact most places are average, and only a very select few will ever be the mad rush you are hoping for. Assuming, then, that you will have to tackle a few rubbish markets in your time there are a few things you can do to make them better and try to push sales.

Serve the Meal they Want

Is it an office area and a midweek lunchtime market? Then those folks want an entire meal. You will find it much easier to sell them a meal than a snack, and depending on area they will be happy to pay for your quality. Consider a deal where you add drinks and a side to your product. If you're in a more industrial area then you need something more filling and possibly cheaper. Load up your carbs and lower your prices, so that you get more physical food for your cash. If you're around during breakfast then get a breakfast offering that compliments your main food, or succumb and do a cheap bacon sarnie until 11.

Evening and weekend markets are much more forgiving, as people will plan to eat from several vendors. You can sell snacks much more readily and sweets will also sell once everyone has had a first course or three. Here you may even want to consider cheap treats: little taster portions that you can bang out for a couple of quid, but watch out: If you are at a street food market then you may miss out on sales because folks can try your food without buying a full size portion.

Samples

Some foods lend themselves to sampling and some don't. Either way, if you want to experiment with this I'd recommend the following:

- Only sample on quiet days. No need to give it away for free if people are happy to pay for it.
- If it's hot food, do it in small batches. No point in letting it go cold.
- Stay inside your unit. You want to be able to convert that sale instantly, rather than having to direct them back to your stall "somewhere over there".
- Don't shout. Potential customers will just give you a wide berth and you will only attract freebie-seekers.
- Wait until you see them looking at your menu. Make direct eye-contact and offer them a sample.

We use samples to secure what might have otherwise been a maybe-sale. But then again our product is comparatively expensive and we want to target it quite specifically. If you have a cheap product (churros are a great example of this) then the scattergun approach is the way forward: address every customer, regardless of how interested they appear, and make sure they try your product.

Overall it's a good way to stimulate slow sales just before lunch, but make sure you can quickly drop free samples as soon as sales pick up.

Discounts

In a lot of cases you match your price to the area you're trading in. If trade is bad, one possible reason is that you're too expensive. By all means fine-tune your price to the area, but I'd be wary of discounts.

If you can discount your product, the thought train goes, it was never worth the higher price in the first place. Charge a guy £2 for your epic battered celery and lamb skewers toady, they are much less likely to want to pay £4 tomorrow. If you are trying to make a market work, discounting is not a great solution. You're better off figuring out exactly what your market wants (see above) and selling that instead.

Reducing the price will almost always lead to reducing your profit, and that's the one thing you don't want to do. However, there are ways to lower your price while increasing your profit, and that's where you might want to have a play. Offering a lower price for multiple purchases will tempt a customer to spend more, so a freebie if they buy a certain number or a discounted price if they buy a combo.

Try to only offer a discount that you would be happy to offer all the time (we do a soup & toastie bundle for a fixed price, for example). I would not even recommend selling off end-of-day toasties cheap unless I was never planning to return. Instead give your food to other traders for swaps or take it home for tea.

The Off Season

If you're in this for the long haul then hopefully you will sail through your first year and be the far side of Christmas before you have a chance to catch a breath. You have then entered the Off-season, which runs from the beginning of January through till around Easter.

There is usually some work available around these times, but it will be slow, cold and dark. Markets will probably still charge you the same amount to show up, but customers will much less keen to eat outdoors.

We shut down fully in January, refuse all work and give the Beast a month to rust a little further into our driveway. It means we have a chance to get the paperwork under control, catch up with friends and have a bit of a break. If you can afford to do it, it's lovely. If you are doing this full time though, chances are that cash flow issues will start to catch up if you spend too long out of action. You also risk losing regular pitches to people who will work in mid-winter. Weirdoes.

If you are trading from a gazebo during this time, you will get cold. Really, really cold. It makes everything hard work, puts you in a bad mood and sucks all the joy out of life. You will need: Thermal undies, lots of layers, good gloves, fingerless gloves, waterproof winter boots with a thick sole, a hot water bottle (if you have a tea urn) and something rubber to stand on. It doesn't make winter trading pleasant, but it makes it almost bearable.

If you do need to work through winter then your best bet are regular markets. There are also occasional corporate gigs available from companies who are busy up until Christmas, and may celebrate afterwards. If you have an all-electric setup you can trade indoors, so pub pop-ups, indoor markets and smaller events could be a good source of income.

Either way, don't panic about getting no work for the first three months of the year (as long as you can get by). It doesn't mean everyone suddenly doesn't like you; it's just that no one really thinks about food, summer or festivals until the New Year's resolutions are thoroughly forgotten. If you are trying to work and failing, invest the time in applications for the summer instead. There's far more money around in the middle of the year, and a great summer is worth a lot more to you that a busy but unprofitable winter.

Working with Other Street Food Traders

It's a small industry, and especially within your area you will end up knowing everyone, at least by reputation. We are all technically in competition, but at the same time we need each other to survive. In my experience street food is one of the friendliest industries to work in, and I think it's in everyone's interests to keep it like that.

Rather than regarding your fellow street food traders as competition, look at them as fighting the same battle as you, on the same side. If we all share information about good and bad events or organisers who should be avoided then everyone benefits.

Direct competition only really exists if you're doing the same food in the same area. If this is the case, and after starting out you realise you have picked the same food as someone nearby, try not to copy their methods. Instead try and find a way to diferntiate and improve on your product, without mimicking their methods. Like it or loathe it, this is a small community, and copycats do not last long.

Safety

I know the paperwork seems like a nightmare, but it's there because otherwise any old idiot with a cooker could serve street food. It also gives you piece of mind. You know your food and equipment is safe because you follow these steps to make sure of it.

So what about when someone really isn't.

I have watched a guy wok-frying over gas, while smoking, with his ashtray and a glass of wine balanced on the gas bottle. The gas hose for that bottle was running directly below the cooking area.

Nothing happened. Things very rarely do, it's just when they do happen people tend to get limbs blown off.

This is why your best bet is going for full compliance. If you do see something terrifying then telling the site manager is your first port of call. If they seem indifferent even after you have shared your concerns then you have the option of calling the local Environmental Health Officer. They will then probably call the site manager, who will know that someone has told on them. Suspicion may well fall on you. Unfortunately this process is far from ideal, but it's the best the industry can currently offer. In the long run, it's probably preferable to winding up scattered in flaming heaps across a field.

If you are concerned and don't want to kick up a fuss then take some pictures, compose factual email and blast it to the EHO as soon as you can. Chances are it won't save you this time, but it may well save someone's skin eventually.

Trader Etiquette

There are no hard and fast rules or secret handshakes, but there are a few things which bother other traders. I'll tell you about them so that you know, and hopefully we can all just be better, nicer people as a result.

5 Minutes

As in "I'll just be 5 minutes mate" when you are blocking access, either in or out of site. Sure, it only feels like 5 minutes to you, because you're busy loading or unloading. It's actually almost certainly more like 15, even if you're quick, because no one can load their full catering setup in 5 minutes. During that 20 minute period the other person can do absolutely nothing. They're probably all packed up (or wanting to pitch up where you're parked, or waiting to unload some distance away) and just want to get on, rather than have to stand over you for 25 minutes while you just really quickly get these last few bits out.

Imagine we actually paid ourselves for our time. 30 minutes of wages is actually a significant amount of cash. So if you do get asked nicely to move then be a mate and shunt you van back a few meters. We'll do the same for you.

Swaps

Especially at festivals you will not want to eat your own food for the entire weekend, and the best way to a varied diet (all 5 of your daily portions of stodge) is to do swaps with other traders. It's customary to come prepared though. Bring cash and offer to pay, but offer swaps at the same time. If they fancy your food and have the authority to make that call - random summer employees may not – then chances are you will get food without paying for it.

Just be aware that employees also might not have a terribly solid grasp on the cost of food stuffs, and may take one round of swaps as a green light to hit your van every time they feel a bit peckish. If they have a large 8-person operation and there are only 2 of you then you may end up seriously out of pocket.

To combat this, specify how many swaps you are willing to offer: A portion for a portion. Things change when you are swapping with mates, but you can probably figure that out for yourselves.

Politics

This is a detestable part of any industry, but becomes especially complex in a small one like ours. Everyone knows everyone else, and we are all in competition for the next great gig or the private hire contract that means you can retire early. We have different opinions and experience with food, with the industry and with event organisers, and it gives us a varying outlook on life.

By politics I mean that people don't always get on. A very small number are not even especially nice. But you end up having to work with all of them, at least once. Most of us just want to make a living, have a fun time and do so without getting in anyone else's way. Those few people who are not too fussed about the final point are the ones that seem to breed drama.

I'm afraid I can't help you manage it. Advice to try and stay out of it would be well heeded by all of us, but the more involved you get, the more people you meet, the greater the likelihood that one of them will turn out to be a devious little toe rag. They exist in all walks of life. Try not to let it get to you.

The List

Every trader has a list of events to visit every year. It's a lot of work to put together, and it represents a good chunk of value to the company. For this reason, we are all fairly cautious about our lists. Don't ask for an in depth guide to a fellow street-fooder's calendar. It's making conversation to ask if they have been anywhere good recently, but it's seriously nosey to ask for events you can trade at. Do your own research, keep your ears open and be nice, people will share information on their own.

Referrals

Once you do start picking up events you will eventually end up with two great events on one weekend, or a wedding enquiry when you already have a festival booked. Passing these jobs to other traders via your recommendation will be helpful to the customer and earn you serious brownie points and referrals back in the opposite direction.

Accountancy

Unless you are an accountant by trade, this part will probably be the bit you are dreading. Don't panic. As a newly formed company you have 18 months before HMRC will harass you for paperwork. If you stay on top of things, get yourself an accountant and try not to panic, this bit is actually just dull, rather than difficult.

Accountancy Basics

The more of this you do yourself, the less it will cost you to pay a bookkeeper and/or accountant. It's a study in data entry. Do the data entry correctly and the end of year becomes a few quick sums over a cup of tea and a biccy. Neglect your data entry and the end of year becomes a stressful pain in the backside. Guess which one most of us opt for?

Yes, naturally we all leave everything till the last minute. It takes a bit of practise to get into good habits with your paperwork.

Step one is to collect your receipts. We then highlight the amount and the date, which will speed up data-entry later. Even if you plan on getting an accountant to tackle everything else, this is where you should start.

Step two is to get an excel spreadsheet template off the internet ("excel accounting template" should throw up some options) and enter your data into this. It needs to include dates, suppliers, amount and a category: equipment, food, vehicle running costs etc.

Step three is to consider spending money on an accountancy programme or an accountant. There are lots of subscription-based

e that will manage most of the workload and produce
ir summaries you need to give to HMRC. They will all
y are the best, most flexible and most stream-lined. I'd
lependent reviews before settling on any one, but they
support who can talk you through the basics and teach
work. Check if they are compatible with other systems,
especially excel. If you ever want to stop using the service, you need
to be able to get your data out at the end.

Step four is to find a good accountant. As your business grows you
will eventually need someone who can reliably process your
paperwork in such a way that HMRC does not feel the need to go
through your bins and get inappropriate with your filing.

As a cash business you are more likely to be on their radar than a
card-processing bricks and mortar restaurant, because in our
industry, money tends to vanish. They are aware of this, they have
algorithms to monitor how much food goes in (your purchases) and
how much food goes out (sales) and they have a good idea of the
money that should be in the middle. Assuming these figures are
healthy and normal, you have nothing to fear.

That is why a good accountant is an excellent find - if you can find
one. There are lots of accountants out there who will process your
books and submit to HMRC, then charge you a small fortune. Finding
one of the ones who will work with you, helping you reduce your
wastage, analyse your takings and increase your profits is the key.
These people don't really need to advertise, because their new clients
are mostly referrals from existing clients.

Ask around once you have established yourself and see who you
can find. Remember you should have 18 months before you first have
to submit anything major to HMRC (if you're not paying yourself) as
you get about 6 months after your yearend to get your affairs in
order.

For the first 3 years of our business we had an excel spreadsheet
and an accountant who processed our spreadsheet, had an annual
meeting with us and then submitted our filing to HMRC and his invoice
to us. It was an amicable enough arrangement, but not especially
proactive. We have since found ourselves a new accountant, through

a recommendation, a new accounting programme (we use Quickbooks) and we are having a much better time.

On the subject of time: occasionally accountants like to charge you for theirs. You have a meeting; they bill you for the pleasure. Those that do are not the kind of accountants you want in the first place, but either way, if they didn't tell you about this in advance you should firmly and calmly tell them to swivel on it.

Payroll

Your accountant will almost certainly be happy to take this off your hands for a regular fee, but if there is only one or two of you, and you are reasonably computer literate, you can have a stab at this yourself.

In April 2013 HMRC finally made it to the 21st century and started allowing employers to process their payroll online. Real Time Information payroll (snazzily abbreviated to RTI) means that each month you tell HMRC what all your employees are up to, rather than having to submit trees and trees of paperwork at the end of each year. I was just starting to run payroll during the changeover, and consequently was doing research into the subject just as all the old skool payroll folks were lamenting the loss of a lifestyle. It sounded unspeakably complicated.

As long as you have the right bits of paper and the correct reference numbers, it really isn't. HMRC themselves provide a programme that will do all the submitting for you if you have 3 employees or fewer, and there are a variety of other private companies who provide a similar free service in the hopes that you will upgrade to their paid-for systems in the future when you expand.

The first step is to sign up as an employer on the HMRC website and get them to send you all the right reference numbers. Select a payroll programme, download it and start adding pieces of information. If you come across a reference number you do not currently have, bear in mind that the dear government do, just occasionally, give the same number two different names. Search "how do I find my [obscure reference number]" and you might realise you already have it.

Alternatively it might just be because HMRC still love sending you things through the post, and that specific one hasn't arrived yet. Some things never change.

If you do find yourself stuck in front of a long, perplexing form with no time and a grim sense of panic setting in, there are tons of guides out on the net that cover this specific programme. You will not be the only person who has got themselves stuck at this particular point. Ask the internet, it will provide. If you can get through this then once you are set up, 15 minutes a month is all you need to make PAYE give you money.

VAT

As a basic rule, hot food is subject to VAT. As another basic rule, ingredients are not. This means that if you are registered for VAT then you can claim back virtually nothing, but have to give the government 20% of your sales. As fun as that sounds, working 20% harder for the good of the government coffers, banker's bonuses and no benefit to you whatsoever is not something you should aspire to.

The VAT threshold changes every year. Searching "current VAT threshold" will give you an accurate idea of where it's at right now. That VAT threshold is the amount of turnover (not profit!) you can make in a rolling 12 month period (so always counting back for the last 365 days). Earn any more than that, even so much as a penny; you should have registered for VAT, and they will come and find you. Once you are registered, you have to pay VAT on everything you sell, not just what you sell past that initial threshold.

In your first year, you can probably ignore it completely. You need to be turning over more than £1500 a week on average to get close, and unless you are nailing street food right from the word go, that probably won't happen.

In your second year and beyond, you do need to start keeping an eye on things. The current 2015/2016 VAT threshold of £82,000 sounds like a lot, but once you take out, well, everything, you are not actually left with a great deal of cash. For this reason you need to look at optimising your business for profit, not for turnover. I've dealt with this earlier, but if you do realise you're regularly hitting over

162

£1500/week but only gathering a net profit of 20p, you need to have a serious think. Losing 20% of what you make to the tax gods could actually see you making a net loss.

A good way to keep track of your turnover is a simple spreadsheet where you put in the details of every event you do, alongside the date. If you can work out how much you spent in pitch fees, food and sundry costs as well that's even better, and you're well on the way to bona fide bookkeeping. After a year has passed you let Excel add up the values. If they are anywhere near the magic number then you need to start looking carefully at your less profitable events, and dropping anything that isn't making you a good return.

Update your spreadsheet on a regular basis and keep checking back to this-time-last-year, so that you can stay below the threshold.

If eventually you do want to expand your business further then there are plenty of people out there happy to give you suggestions on the best way to stay below the threshold. These usually involve some form of second company, and a division of labour, costs and time between the two. The legality of these enterprises is a minefield, and if you want to go down that route I would strongly advise seeking professional advice. I have sort much, and mostly been rewarded with conflicting views that don't give me much reassurance.

Expansion

Getting on for 5 years down the line we look back at street food and feel like we have pretty much mastered it. There will always be ups and downs, the Beast will always be a probable MOT failure and toasties will always be "the next big thing" but never quite "the big thing we want to eat right now". We have encountered every single conceivable problem and, thankfully, have survived them all.

Looking forward to our next season is now very reminiscent of looking back at our last. Many of the same events, which is great and profitable, but no new challenges. Fans of the quiet life probably won't understand what I mean, but while street food is an ever-changing, fickle and weather-dependent beast, the coping methods remain the same.

So what of our next challenge? It's really a question of what street food sets you up for. All those bizarre skills must be good for something.

Setting up a New Venture

Setting up a company was dead hard 4 years ago. Luckily, that was 4 years ago, before we had experience setting up a company. We are now all the proud owners of the surprisingly transferable skill of "setting up and running a company" along with "not being terrified of self-employment". There are plenty of new careers out there just waiting for an entrepreneur with enough enthusiasm and drive to get a street food business off the ground. Realistically, I haven't made 25,000 toasties just to leave all that and cut my ties with street food. So I'm going to stick with the options that are most suited to the next logical step.

A Second Unit

This is probably the easiest option, because if you're anything like us you probably have half a second unit accumulated already. You may choose to upgrade to a van, or get an electric setup for indoor gigs, or just duplicate what you already have.

The Van or Trailer:

If you are not already the owner of a van you may not appreciate how quick they are to set up and relocate. They are much easier on the back than a gazebo or build-up and they are a draw if they're reasonably cool. So you may have your eye on one, which would be sensible. You also have the benefit, unlike many new starters out there, of knowing exactly what you will sell and how you will sell it. Make sure you get a van that is optimised for your setup. See the section on vans for more details.

The Electric Setup:

Trading indoors will make the winter much more pleasant, and give you access to some markets that van-based traders only dream of. Just try and keep your electricity consumption to a minimum, so that you have maximum versatility regarding events.

The Duplicate

Never turn down another booking! There are definitely advantages to having a whole second setup, even if it isn't out regularly. If you are not planning on taking this one on regular outings then I'd steer clear of a van, as that sucker has to be taxed, MOTed and insured to be useful. Having two gazebo-based units should make you mega versatile; you just have to decide which one you will be working in, and how you can possibly bear to let the other out of your sight.

The Secondary Speciality

If you regularly attend festivals, it's worth considering offering another, totally distinct food choice. You can then theoretically attend one festival with two units, and make twice as much for (hopefully) less than double the work. You can also supervise both, which is a bonus for us control freaks.

Event Organisation

How hard can it be? Having attended hundreds of badly run events over the years you can get a feel for how something should be run. So surely you can do better. The in-depth version of this topic is a whole new book, but just trust me that it isn't as easy as it looks.

The biggest challenge will always be getting folks to show up, and that is something that we, as street food traders, have never had to worry about. We just moan to the organisers when they don't. Some skills are useful though: you are embedded in the local food culture, and possibly have a good following of relevant foodies already. You know what events are currently going on where, and may have spotted a gap in the market.

Now you just need to find a location, secure the right to use it, find a suitable style of event, book traders, get insurance, find out if there are any other applicable licenses, perform a risk assessment, plan and book entertainment, consider lighting, security, maximum capacity, waste disposal & recycling, parking, toilets, power, layout, wet weather contingency and seating.

That's the easy bit. The hard bit is getting people to show up.

As part of Scoff we organised several events with varying degrees of success. The big unknown will always be people. Unless you can somehow sell tickets in advance (see pop-ups), there will always be that worry: what if NO ONE shows up.

Pop-Ups

This is not necessarily part of an expansion, but it is a new angle you can add to the business. You take over a restaurant for the day/week/night and serve your food from their kitchen. The big bonus here is that you can sell tickets in advance, giving you accurate numbers on the night and no wastage. The downside is that certain foods do not lend themselves to a pop up. That may just be me, purveyor of breath-takingly good but not really popup-suited toasties.

You may also find (the experience-worn cynic within would like to add) that you put the work into establishing a pop-up, getting a following and promoting the event. Then the pub owner realises they could just as easily do it themselves and kicks you out. The sly pub owner may even nudge the price up gently until you quit of your own accord. That way no one ever needs to have one of those messy, confrontational conversations.

Street Food Collective

This is a group of street food folks who get together, the idea being that you have strength in numbers. You can then put on events, provide advice or generally share jobs. There is a lot of effort involved in setting up a collective and no guarantee of success. Plus you either need someone to be in charge or you all need to be setting the collective up for the same reason.

Let me give you an example. You want to start a collective so that you can win awards, put on great events and people will think you're great, raising the profile of your Cornbread 'N Gravy stall.

Your fellow members want to start a collective to generate more trading opportunities for themselves, where they don't have to pay pitch fees. Then all the stuff you just mentioned, sure.

Both of these are excellent reasons to start a collective. But you may well end up working towards different goals, as you try and create that perfect showpiece event, while they try and generate as much work as possible. You then realise that someone else is being praised for work you did, and no one is keeping you in the loop. It all happens, none of it intentionally. This is the curse of the committee.

My three top tips are:

- Expect to disagree. Maybe not straight away, but eventually. Agree how you will solve these problems when they come up (talking about them works best).
- Actively try and stay friends. It takes work and patience. You will understand when you get there.
- Agree on what the collective priorities are. If these are not your priorities, you may not be able to make this work and could save yourself a LOT of work by stepping away early.

Bricks and Mortar

This is the biggest, most expensive form of expansion. You will be staggered at how expensive it actually is. While street food runs on high hopes, this runs on cold, hard cash and hours that make your supposedly busy life on the road look like a Centre Parcs holiday.

The thing that might eventually push you towards the end of your nomadic food-based lifestyle is the inherent uncertainty of it all. No matter how long you work for, how good you research is, there will always be a painfully bad festival just around the corner waiting to blindside you. Until the industry allows us to fight back there is always a risk this might happen.

It's also not a sport that lends itself to babies. Not that sproglets are everyone's cup of tea, but standing in a confined space for 17 hours a day will not be pleasant with a stomach the size of Norfolk. A restaurant is not necessarily an easier option for a mum-to-be, but at least it's easier to employ staff for when you go on maternity/paternity leave.

The how-toos of running a restaurant are a whole book to themselves, but if that is where you're going then street food is probably the best dry run you could hope for, because it doesn't just give you all the management skills, which you would get from actually working in the restaurant industry, it also gives you the back office business understanding, which is arguably more important.

Compared to street food this is not an easy life. You need a lot more money, a lot more time to make a profit and a lot less life around the edges. It's worth speaking to other street food traders and noting how many used to own a restaurant. It may not be the same across the board, but it's surprising how many have ditched the bricks and mortar.

So Here We Are Then.

Hopefully that gives you enough inspiration and information to want to have a stab at starting your own business. If you do manage to make a success of it, please tell us; we'd love to hear from you.

Whatever you decide, whether it's a street food empire or one, perfect unit, I wish you all the success in the world. Keep it fun, do what you love and be safe.

Right: hands in the middle ... Go street food!

Further Information

If you don't already follow the blog: www.thejabberwocky.co.uk/blog, it's a great place to start. We update regularly with random articles and also answer questions on everything street food related.

http://www.streetfood.org.uk/ is administered by NCASS. They represent the industry, but don't actively trade. They can offer solid advice on legalities, but you need to be a member to be able to ask them for advice in person.

Twitter #streetfood. This is where you will find everyone.

The web at large. There are general articles that will give you much of the same advice found here, but specifics are still fairly rare.

Other books. Most of them are for a US audience, and have some interesting thoughts, but are not really relevant over here. Health codes and trading permits are entirely different across the pond, as are attitudes to street food.

Getting out and about. You can come and visit us somewhere near Leamington Spa. If it's quiet we'll be happy to chat and give you some pointers. Alternatively just find some street food events nearby and talk to people, try the food and soak up the ambiance.

BUSINESS GATEWAY PORTREE   CORN DOG
   TIGH NA SGIRE   DOG ON A LOG
   PARK LANE   FROG ON A LOG
   PORTREE
   IUSI 9EP
   01478 698316

forté
"Midge bites"

HAIRY KNEES

KILT.

NAMES ??

FOODNESS ME
BURGER NESS.
BURGER ME ! *
BUN ON THE RUN .
JUICY BUNS .
'MIDGY BITES' *

22179735R00095

Printed in Great Britain
by Amazon